A MAN'S GUIDE TO PARTNER BETRAYAL

A MAN'S GUIDE TO PARTNER BETRAYAL

Overcoming the Pain and Repercussions of a Cheating Partner

Adam B. Nisenson, LMFT, CSAT

SANO PRESS, LLC
CLAREMONT, CA

1st Edition

DISCLAIMER

The information provided in this book is for educational purposes only and should NOT be considered a substitute for professional medical or health advice. It is not intended to replace professional diagnosis treatment or guidance. The content is based on general knowledge, the author's personal experiences, and the author's research, but may not be applicable to individual circumstances. The author and publisher are not liable for any actions taken based on the information presented. Consult a qualified healthcare professional for personalized medical advice and treatment.

ISBN-13: 978-1-956620-06-1

ABOUT THIS BOOK

I intentionally and unapologetically created this book for men. Its purpose is to acknowledge the glaring gap in resources available to men experiencing partner betrayal trauma. It does so in a language and perspective to which men can instinctively relate. Experiencing partner betrayal is complex. Expectations and other barriers are challenging, affecting one's vulnerability often in dysfunctional ways.

As a Licensed Marriage and Family Therapist and Certified Sex Addiction Therapist who has personally experienced the impact of partner betrayal and infidelity from my then-wife, I infused this book with both my expertise and personal understanding. In this way, I can connect your experiences as a man and provide help to those facing betrayal with depth and nuance.

Please know that these pages go beyond being a compilation of resources. They are meant to be your practical path toward healing, support, solidarity, and empathy. Men, you are navigating a difficult journey, and I promise to show you that you are not alone.

In healing,

—Adam B. Nisenson, LMFT, CSAT

CAROL JUERGENSEN SHEETS LCSW, CCPS-S, PCC, CSAT-S

Although it has been around since the beginning of time, sexual addiction is an epidemic. Once the internet became well established, it gave people open availability to be unfaithful, compulsive, and pleasure-seeking. It made addiction accessible.

When I started in this field, there were no programs for partners and very few resources for the man who had problematic sexual behavior or for the partner who was experiencing betrayal trauma. As the profession of sex addiction became more specialized, we learned much about how to treat male sex addicts and female partners.

Our profession has done an excellent job of creating programming and treatment to address male sex addiction and female partner betrayal; however, we consistently hear from men that there are very few resources available to walk them through the betrayal journey. We see a major lack of therapeutic understanding or treatment for male partners who have experienced sexual betrayal trauma.

The good news is that male partners now have a guidebook to assist them through betrayal trauma. Adam B. Nisenson has written a brilliant book on Masculine

Betrayal Trauma Recovery and has developed a model that will assist male partners in understanding why this has been such a silent epidemic with few men having the words to describe how wounding this has been to their sense of self. Nisenson has delved into the seven stages that men may experience as they navigate through the pain and depth of their wounding. He gives hope to the experience by showing men how to find their own post-traumatic growth by teaching them the steps to understanding their very own personal trauma experience and how to grow from it.

Adam Nisenson's **Masculine Betrayal Trauma Recovery Model** encompasses a safety plan that ensures men will not have to navigate partner betrayal alone but will have a guidebook that offers solid advice to consider while on the path to healing. He encourages you to explore your own feelings and honor the process of working through the trauma and one's own ego to get to the other side.

His Seven Stages of MBT Recovery will gently encourage you to do a deep dive into the normal reactions you have experienced because you are a man who has been socialized to deal with trauma and injury by hiding your feelings and seeking out rivalry instead.

This model will encourage awareness, insight, and constructive compassion as you explore your feelings and gain clarity into your healing.

You can get through this and grow, and the MBT Recovery Model will show you how to gain resilience and self-worth from this painful experience!

A big thank you to Adam for recognizing the huge gap in education, insight, and resources for men who have had to navigate this journey on their own. This book will be a game changer for how we as professionals help men who have been betrayed and as a personal roadmap for you to start your own betrayal recovery.

—*Carol Juergensen Sheets*, LCSW, CCPS-S, PCC, CSAT-S

Carol is the author of *Help.Her.Heal: An Empathy Workbook for Sex Addicts to Help Their Partners Heal* and *Help. Them.Heal: Teaching You Both How to Heal Your Relationship After Sexual Betrayal.* She is the co-author of *Transformations: A Woman's Journey of Self-Discovery* and *Unleashing Your Power: Moving Through the Trauma of Partner Betrayal.*

TABLE OF CONTENTS

WELCOME AND SORRY YOU'RE HERE

HOW DID WE GET HERE?

You're standing at a crossroads, a place I know all too well from my own experience. It's a junction where the shadows of betrayal stretch long and deep, casting a shroud over what once was a bright outlook. Like you, I've walked this path, navigating through the fog of disbelief and the sharp stings of partner betrayal. My odyssey, sparked by the betrayal of my then-wife over 13 years ago, didn't just alter my professional trajectory; it ushered me into a fraternity of men who bear the silent, searing wounds of partner infidelity.

In those moments of stark vulnerability, my world was cloaked in grief and seething anger that seemed foreign, yet painfully mine. I reached out for a lifeline, only to find that the support structures in place were largely tailored for women, rendering my pain seemingly invisible and my journey painfully solitary. Society's blueprint for masculinity—with its stern tone to remain unflinching and stoic—only served to amplify the echoes of my solitude. It felt like I was navigating uncharted territory where the guides were few and the paths unmarked.

And yet, while I was in the throes of this turmoil, I discovered a truth so eloquently captured by bestselling author and psychotherapist Esther Perel: "Betrayal comes in many forms. It can range from the egregious to the subtlest of disappointments." This realization became the genesis of this book—a testament and guide born from the chasms of my despair and the resolve to shine a light for others treading this rugged terrain.

This book is more than a collection of pages commiserating with readers who share similar experiences. It chronicles a journey emerging from darkness and woven threads of pain to resilience and an unwavering pursuit of healing. It's a narrative that seeks to validate the silent battles, bridge the void where resources are scarce, and offer a sanctuary where your pain is seen, your struggles acknowledged, and your journey toward healing honored.

Within these chapters lies an exploration of the labyrinth of betrayal trauma—a deep dive into its complexities and nuances. We will challenge prevailing narratives that silence male voices in conversations about betrayal and pain. Together, we will embark on this expedition of self-discovery and healing, acknowledging that while the pain of partner betrayal is a stark reality, it also holds the potential to be the crucible from which a stronger, more resilient self can emerge.

As you dive into these pages, remember you're not alone in this journey. You are part of a community united by shared pain and by our determination to emerge from the shadows to understand, heal, and grow. Welcome to your path of transformation, where every step—no matter how uncertain—is a stride toward a horizon of hope, understanding, and renewed strength.

THE MALE EGO

In the realm of what I call MBT Recovery™ (Masculine Betrayal Trauma Recovery), the ego is more than a harmless layer. It lies at the core of your self-image and is deeply intertwined with your sense of worth and identity. When betrayal strikes, it doesn't just cause pain; it shakes the foundation of how you perceive yourself. This profound impact leads you to question:

- How does partner betrayal reshape my view of myself?

- How do societal norms about masculinity shape and sometimes warp my personal experiences during this trauma?

Let's explore these questions together. I'm not just talking about concepts; I'm diving deep into the core struggles that many men silently endure. The ego—often misunderstood as a display of toughness—is actually an expansive aspect of your being. It encompasses how you perceive yourself in relation to the world—your worth, capabilities, and accomplishments. Betrayal challenges these perceptions, often leading to a sometimes painful reassessment.

Understanding the role of the ego in your healing journey is pivotal. You'll tackle the ingrained expectations that dictate how we, as men, are "supposed" to react to emotional wounds. You will begin to see how these expectations can block your path to healing by setting up barriers against expressing vulnerability and seeking support. By confronting and understanding these societal barriers, you will forge your path toward recovery.

But your exploration of the ego doesn't stop simply because you now understand the impact of betrayal. There's a necessary process of rebuilding and redefining yourself once you emerge from the storm. You will begin to see a stronger and more resilient sense of self. You will learn to embrace both your strength and your vulnerability as integral parts of your masculinity. This journey is so much more than overcoming partner betrayal. It's about growth and emotional maturity. Navigating the ego is like walking through a battlefield and, at the same time, tending to your wounds.

STAGES OF NAVIGATING BETRAYAL

The essence of healing Masculine Betrayal Trauma lies in understanding its seven stages. These stages don't follow any particular path; they simply represent a range of psychological states men tend to encounter. From shock and pain to nurturing strength and personal growth, each stage offers its unique insights and practical guidance.

This journey entails more than progressing from one stage to another as if tackling a checklist. The focus is on your personal transformation and development. As David Richo insightfully points out, "Our greatest fear isn't that we are inadequate, but that we hold power beyond measure." As you journey through these pages, you'll tap into that power—the power to heal, grow, and redefine who you are in the aftermath of betrayal.

This book is not so much a guide as it is your companion during your personal expedition through the trauma experience. It stands as a testament to the resilience within you—each of you. As you turn each page, keep in mind that this journey is uniquely yours. You have the power to shape it, to make it your own. Even in the darkest moments of betrayal, there's a path leading to clarity, understanding, and renewed strength.

Welcome to your journey of self-discovery and path through partner betrayal, where resilience and transformation come together and every step forward is a testimony to your strength and a stride toward becoming a more empowered version of yourself.

DEFINITIONS

MBT RECOVERY™: A DEEP DIVE

Masculine Betrayal Trauma Recovery—also known as MBT Recovery™—is a term I've coined to encapsulate the turmoil experienced by men when confronted with partner infidelity. It encompasses a blend of shock, disbelief, and a deep sense of betrayal that gnaws at one's self-perception and challenges one's ego. MBT Recovery™ goes beyond surface-level impact; it unpacks emotions such as anger, jealousy, and competitiveness—all wrapped up with cultural expectations surrounding masculinity.

Navigating through MBT Recovery™ involves navigating self-doubt and questioning your value. It requires confronting moments of silence, withdrawal from decreased productivity, and struggles in expressing vulnerability. It's a reevaluation of self, a rekindling of resilience, and a quest to reconcile deeply ingrained notions of masculinity making positive use of the raw, vulnerable human experience of betrayal.

GENDER, PRONOUNS, AND PERSPECTIVES

While I've written this book from a male perspective, partner betrayal knows no gender. It's a human ordeal, and the betrayer could be anyone, irrespective of gender. So, whether you relate to terms like "spouse," "partner," or "betrayer," the essence of the experience remains universal: a sense of trust is broken followed by a journey toward healing.

BETRAYAL PARTNER: THE WOUNDED WARRIOR

In this narrative, the betrayal partner is you—a man who has felt the earth-shattering impact of infidelity. It signifies more than just being betrayed. It represents strength, vulnerability, and the courage to rise from the ashes of broken trust. Whether it's emotional or physical infidelity, the betrayal experienced sets the betrayed on a path—a path of complex emotions and a quest for healing and understanding.

BETRAYER: THE CATALYST OF PAIN

The betrayer is the one who stepped outside the sacred bounds of trust, shattering the foundation of the relationship. This term isn't about scrutinizing the infidelity itself; it's about the aftermath, psychological trauma, and trust that now lies in fragments. Understanding the dynamics of betrayal is key to navigating through the pain and toward healing.

INFIDELITY, PHYSICAL AFFAIRS, AND EMOTIONAL AFFAIRS: THE MANY FACES OF BETRAYAL

Infidelity isn't a monolith; it is more than one interlocking piece—from the physical affairs that breach the sanctity of a relationship to the emotional affairs that silently erode the foundation of trust and intimacy. Each form, each instance of infidelity, is a blow to the heart, a challenge to the soul, and a call to engage in healing, understanding, and growth.

DISCLAIMER

A WORD TO THE WISE: THE ROLE OF THIS BOOK

This book is a compass, a guide through the tumultuous journey of partner betrayal. It's not a substitute for professional advice but a collection of insights, a source of support, and a ray of hope. As you navigate through these pages and read these words, remember to seek guidance, listen to your heart, and tread the path of healing with patience, courage, and an open mind. Your journey is your own, unique in its pain and profound in its potential for growth and rediscovery.

Chapter 1:

THE SILENT STRUGGLE

As a man grappling with your partner's infidelity, you often must navigate a path filled with silence and uncertainty. Unfortunately, society equates masculinity with strength and emotional resilience, which means you might keep your struggles to yourself, but behind this façade lies a deep, heavy truth. The emotional upheaval and heartbreak you experience after being betrayed in a relationship often leads to suffering silently, where you crave support and recognition yet have nowhere to turn.

Throughout history, the focus on infidelity has been predominantly on females as the victims of betrayal and heartache. While this perspective is valid, it unintentionally overlooks the anguish felt by men caught in the same storm of betrayal. This gap in understanding is an imbalance that only perpetuates society's discomfort with men showing vulnerability. Because men don't often report being betrayed by their partners, they remain silent about those experiences.

CONFRONTING SOCIETAL EXPECTATIONS

I get the pressure you might be experiencing. You're expected to show resilience when faced with adversity, which feels heavy—like you're carrying the weight of the world. This deeply ingrained expectation keeps you from expressing pain or seeking help because you don't want to admit to others what you consider weakness. As a result, you often feel isolated in your struggles, believing you must fight your battles alone. In her book *Daring Greatly*, Brené Brown, renowned for her research on vulnerability and shame states, "Vulnerability is not winning or losing; it's having the courage to show up and be seen when we have no control over the outcome. Vulnerability is not weakness; it's our greatest measure of courage." Embrace this insight, and you can take the first step toward breaking down the unnecessary and self-imposed barriers of expectations. You will discover there's strength in vulnerability and solidarity through shared experiences.

THE HIDDEN BATTLE WITHIN

Dealing with infidelity brings turmoil. You hide your internal chaos from others. You put on a mask of normality as you continue to fulfill your roles as a partner, father, and professional while silently grappling with your crumbling world. The lack of spaces where your pain can be acknowledged or expressed only adds to the burden you carry, making healing more challenging and complex.

The first hurdle in addressing the impact of infidelity is recognizing that your pain is deep and valid. Your silence about it is your choice, but that choice often originates from a narrative that lays out how men should handle their emotional wounds.

As you embark on healing and recovery, it's important to admit and express your emotions in a safe environment. This expression could involve confiding in a trusted friend, joining support groups with others who have gone through similar experiences, or seeking guidance from a counselor. Opening up is a step toward validating your feelings and initiating the healing process. I will talk more in future chapters about sharing, being vulnerable, and finding ways of not going on this journey alone.

Equally important is developing strategies to cope with the pain of partner betrayal. Engaging in activities provides an outlet for your emotions. Exercise, practicing mindfulness, playing sports, hiking, meditation, yoga, or art are all incredibly helpful. They act as valves for releasing pent-up emotions and stress, and they offer relief and an opportunity to reconnect with yourself on a new level.

Redefining your understanding of strength and masculinity can also be profoundly therapeutic. Embracing vulnerability as an act of courage rather than weakness allows you to break free from stereotypes that can discourage you from seeking support. Any shift in this direction can enable you to more fully embrace your humanness with all its complexities and emotions.

Lastly, give yourself time and permission to heal. Healing from partner betrayal isn't a straight line or a quick trip. Expect ups and downs, setbacks, and progress. Be patient with yourself and the healing process; it takes time. During that time, you're allowing yourself to experience a range of emotions without judgment. These are monumental steps toward healing.

THE SHATTERED SELF: REFLECTIONS OF A BROKEN MIRROR

Infidelity leaves an imprint on a man's core identity, leaving behind reflections that feel unfamiliar. More than a superficial wound, it goes beyond breaching trust and erodes the foundation of how you might perceive yourself. Like looking at a shattered mirror, the pieces reflect fragments of pain, doubt, and confusion that begin shaping your reality.

For many men, self-worth is closely linked to their relationships. In a relationship, you might view yourself as a combination of protector, provider, and partner. Infidelity violates those roles. It's not the relationship that suffers the betrayal but your perception of who you are. You are having an identity crisis that triggers feelings of inadequacy and defeat.

NAVIGATING THE MAZE OF EMOTIONS

Coping in the aftermath of infidelity involves more than acknowledging the possible end of a relationship—you are navigating through a flurry of emotions. Anger, sadness, confusion, and sometimes even relief combine to create a confusing terrain. The pressure to hide your emotions behind a calm façade deprives you of the space you need to process your feelings. This prolongs your mental healing process as well as your physical well-being. Healing from infidelity is a process of overcoming the inflicted pain and growth and an opportunity to redefine your values, reshape your beliefs about relationships, and ultimately gain an understanding of yourself.

THE JOURNEY OF SELF REDISCOVERY

Moving forward involves more than just rebuilding your self-image; it requires discovering a new sense of identity beyond the experience of betrayal. You are navigating new pathways toward healing and personal development and adopting different perspectives and new ways of being. This journey is not about returning to the way you were before the betrayal but progressing toward a new sense of self-awareness and authenticity.

In the upcoming chapters, I will explore strategies for coping with the emotional turmoil caused by partner betrayal. We will also explore rebuilding self-confidence, examining its impact on your sense of self-worth, and redefining masculinity after experiencing infidelity. Rather than being able to say you've gotten over it and recovered, this journey offers the opportunity to rediscover yourself, emerging stronger, wiser, and more aligned with who you truly are.

MY EXPERIENCE

I want to peel back the layers of my own story, a narrative not defined by someone else's choices but by the impact those choices had on me. It's a tale not of blame but of understanding and growth. When my then-wife entered into a long-term affair, the world as I knew it was turned upside down. But this book—and my journey—isn't about her actions; it's about the wake it left in my life and how I navigated those troubling times.

The betrayal I faced was a stark revelation, illuminating that I was already among the walking wounded before the affair even came to light. As it turned out, my life was built on a shaky foundation, riddled with gaps I had ignored for a long time. Though the betrayal was hers, the cracks in our relationship weren't solely of her making. My complacency, reluctance to demand more from our partnership, and deep-seated fear of truly being seen and possibly hurt all contributed to the storm that eventually broke us.

We all bring baggage into our relationships, and mine was a suitcase packed with doubts about my worthiness of love and an avoidant streak that kept me at arm's length from true intimacy. The irony is that this very hurt, this seismic upheaval in my life, jolted me awake and set me on a new path.

I'm sharing a piece of history of my silent struggle to illustrate how a man might suffer in isolation post-betrayal. It's important to shed light on the pain, confusion, and journey toward healing. My experience and professional insights as a therapist working with individuals who have betrayed and been betrayed offer a unique vantage point. Yes, navigating the intricacies of betrayal from both sides of the fence is complex. But it's also incredibly rewarding to know that my journey filled with pain, enlightenment, and ultimately, transformation can offer hope and guidance to others on both sides walking this path.

QUESTIONS FOR NAVIGATING BETRAYAL

The following questions are meant to guide you through introspection and the process of self-discovery. Writing down your answers in a journal as you work with these questions might be helpful, allowing yourself to express your thoughts and emotions openly.

To be clear, answering these questions isn't about finding fixes. Instead, it's about understanding and healing, permitting yourself to acknowledge your emotions, exploring deeper inquiries, and growing. Each question can be seen as an opening that's leading you toward a deeper awareness of your situation that will reshape how you feel about it and thereby modify your story.

Remember, healing from partner betrayal is unique and personal. There is no right or wrong way to navigate it, only the way that resonates most deeply with you. Allow yourself to take this inventory at your own pace, accepting each question as an opportunity for growth and rediscovery.

1. Acknowledging the pain: What are the main emotions I am feeling right now, and how can I allow myself to fully experience and express them?

2. Challenging social norms: In what ways have societal expectations about masculinity influenced my response to this betrayal?

3. Seeking support: Who in my life can I trust to talk openly about my feelings without fear of judgment or shame?

4. Revisiting identity: How has this experience of betrayal affected my perception of myself as a partner, provider, or protector?

5. Exploring emotions: What complex emotions am I struggling with, and how can I give them space to manifest and be understood?

6. Redefining strength: How can I redefine strength in my life to include vulnerability and emotional openness?

7. Embracing self-compassion: What steps can I take to practice self-compassion and kindness during this challenging time?

8. Finding Healthy Outlets: What activities or hobbies can I engage in that will provide a healthy outlet for my emotions?

9. Redefining relationships: How do I envision my future relationships, and what values and beliefs do I want to bring into them?

10. Creating a new self-image: What aspects of my identity and self-image do I want to retain, and what do I want to redefine or let go of?

Chapter 2:

MANAGING THE CRISIS

After discovering your partner's infidelity, you were probably engulfed in a storm of emotions. The solid foundation of trust the two of you once stood upon has crumbled. You might be looking around and see a dismal landscape of uncertainty and anguish, marked by feelings ranging from disbelief to burning anger and confusion. How do you get past your initial reactions and challenges? Look at this chapter as if you have just discovered a new technology that acts like a navigating device specifically designed for you and your tumultuous journey.

SHOCK, ANGER, AND CONFUSION

A cascade of intense emotions often marks the onset of partner betrayal trauma. Initially, it's common to experience shock—a state characterized by disbelief and numbness. "How could this happen?" reverberates in your mind, reflecting a sense of disbelief. Ironically, shock can be comforting and protective. It acts as a shield to momentarily help you cope with the impact. It serves as your mind's way of pausing and granting you time to process a painful reality.

However, shock dissipates over time, making way for an upsurge of anger. Your anger arises from feelings of hurt and betrayal fueled by your sense of injustice that trust has been violated. The intensity of emotions can catch you off guard, and its strength can surprise you.

Shock, anger, and confusion can mix together in a whirlwind of feelings. Questions about the past and uncertainties about the future shake your trust in your partner as well as others and your judgment, but that's okay. This trio of emotions sets the stage for healing—if you're willing to do some work.

When you express your emotions, you are in effect processing them, and the result is gaining perspective. Seeking guidance from a therapist or betrayal coach can help you uncover even more revelations, insights, and strategies for navigating those feelings. During alone time, do some self-reflection by dedicating moments for introspection. Go for a walk, listen to your favorite music, meditate, or pursue a hobby. These moments of respite can offer healing relief from turmoil, allowing you to find inner calm while giving you space to feel your emotions.

Educate yourself about trauma responses, not just yours but those of others, to better understand their possible impact on your daily life. This knowledge will help put your emotions into context, making them feel less overwhelming and more manageable. You will discover important lessons, like not making decisions in the heat of shock and anger, even though it may seem tempting at the time. Give yourself space and time before committing to your choices because they can have lasting consequences.

Navigating through the trifecta of shock, anger, and confusion following betrayal is different for everyone. You are discovering coping strategies that resonate with you, not what someone else says is helpful. Remember, this path is about gaining insights into yourself and how you uniquely interact with the world around you. Allow yourself the grace of time as a healing medium, and don't adhere to timelines. Every small step forward and moment of self-awareness brings you closer to recovery and self-discovery.

Recognize that your journey may include setbacks and challenges along the way. These are not failures but natural parts of the healing process. Embrace these moments as opportunities for growth and learning, and celebrate the smallest moments of progress you make. As you do so, you will realize that your healing isn't like recovering from a physical wound but about accepting the ups, downs, and the slowly revealed discoveries that eventually lead to resilience, inner strength, and a renewed sense of self.

Your journey through shock, anger, and confusion—no matter how tentative—is evidence to your resilience and capacity for healing, courage, and determination. By facing these challenging emotions head-on and seeking methods to process and manage them, you are laying the groundwork for a future where you can approach life with greater clarity, purpose, and emotional wisdom.

PRACTICAL ADVICE

1. Acknowledge and accept your emotions: Recognize that shock, anger, and confusion are natural, valid responses to betrayal. Acknowledging these emotions is the first step in processing them.

2. Journal for clarity: Writing can be a powerful tool for unburdening your thoughts and feelings in a structured way. Journaling allows you to articulate your emotions, providing clarity and a sense of release, a place to untangle the complex web of your feelings and reactions. It can be particularly helpful in identifying patterns in your thoughts and emotions, leading to greater self-awareness and problem-solving.

3. Physical activity: Engaging in physical activities such as sports or other physical exercise can be an

effective way to channel your anger and reduce stress. Physical exertion can release endorphins, improving your mood and helping to clear your mind.

4. Mindfulness and meditation: Getting in touch with your inner world through practices like mindfulness and meditation can help you manage the intensity of your emotions. They encourage a state of awareness and calm presence in-the-now, allowing you to practice observing your feelings without being overwhelmed by them.

5. Seek trusted support: Talking to a trusted friend, family member, therapist, or betrayal trauma coach is an opportunity to connect with a safe outlet for your emotions. Sometimes, talking to friends or family members who understand your situation and can offer unbiased advice can be helpful. Choose to confide in those who have your best interests at heart and who can provide a different perspective. Verbalizing your feelings to someone else can also give you a new perspective. A specialist can offer professional guidance and strategies to navigate through your challenging emotions. Therapy is a safe space to explore the impact of the betrayal on your self-esteem and personal identity.

6. Consider all options: Reflect on the possible paths forward with your relationship. This reflection might include couples therapy to work on the relationship, a period of separation to gain perspective, or, in some cases, considering the end of the relationship. Each option should be weighed with care and consideration for your long-term emotional health.

7. Take care of physical health: In times of emotional stress, physical health can often be neglected. Pay attention to basic needs like nutrition, sleep, and exercise. A healthy body can support a healthy mind, making it easier to deal with emotional challenges.

8. Avoid isolation: While introspection is important, isolation can also be detrimental. Make an effort to maintain social connections and activities that bring you joy and comfort.

9. Embrace reflection: Allow yourself moments of quiet reflection. This could be walking through a park, hiking a trail, taking part in some other outdoor space in nature, listening to music, or simply sitting in a quiet space. These moments can provide a break from the intensity of your emotions, setting aside specific times for introspection and calming your mind. This is a time to think about what you truly want and need separate from the immediate emotional reactions to the betrayal.

10. Set boundaries for healing: If you're considering staying in the relationship, set clear boundaries with your partner about what you need for healing. This might include working toward more honest communication, transparency, or specific actions to rebuild trust. In Chapter 3, I explain how to set boundaries in detail. Read this chapter before you move forward with any boundaries regarding your situation.

11. Educate yourself about trauma responses: Understanding the psychological impact of betrayal can help you make sense of your emotions and remove some of your fears. Reading about trauma responses and recovery can provide context to what you're experiencing, making them feel less upsetting and more manageable.

12. Avoid rash decisions: Amid shock and anger, it's easy to make impulsive decisions. Give yourself time and space before making significant choices or plans, especially those that may have long-term implications.

13. Be patient with the process: Recognize that understanding and decision-making in the wake of betrayal is a process that takes time. Be patient with yourself, and don't feel pressured to come to quick resolutions.

WHAT COMES NEXT

Once the initial intensity of shock, anger, and confusion begin to subside, what's next? Are there tasks or exercises you should perform? The aftermath of betrayal requires reflection and introspection. You will soon be at the beginning stages of formulating decisions about your relationships and well-being.

Understand that this isn't the time for rushing into decisions. The emotional turmoil can still cloud your judgment and lead to choices that may not align with your long-term well-being or values. Take moments to pause, allowing yourself some time to process what has happened and reflect on the significance of the betrayal in the context of your life and relationships.

Prioritizing your well-being and peace of mind is essential as you navigate the "what comes next" phase, which is a repeating theme throughout this book. I bring it up often because it's so important to remind yourself that you will want to make informed, thoughtful decisions that align with your values, and needs. These decisions will daisy-chain into your new life where you can start to really believe that long-term happiness is possible. Take each day as a separate chunk of time that doesn't have to build flawlessly onto the previous day. Backsliding can and probably will occur, but you will forgive and start again, knowing that you are circling in an overall corrective direction. Trust that with time, reflection, and support, you will find the path that's right for you.

REGAINING EMOTIONAL AND PHYSICAL STABILITY

The experience of betrayal can make you feel upended in a world you don't understand the way you used to. It impacts both your emotional well-being and your sense of physical stability. This upheaval can disrupt your sense of safety and security—cornerstones of a healthy and balanced life. In the wake of a disturbance, regaining your sense of stability becomes vital to your healing process. You are working toward reconstructing a sense of normality and protection amidst the chaos. There's a close relationship between physical and emotional stability. To reclaim the physical, you have to reclaim the emotional. This speaks to your mental health, which is built on a foundation that you'll be reestablishing—a foundation upon which you will rebuild your life, piece by piece, day by day.

PRACTICAL ADVICE

1.   Establish daily routines: Structured daily routines can be incredibly grounding. This might include

setting regular mealtimes, a consistent sleep schedule, and dedicated times for work and relaxation. Routines can provide a sense of control and normality in your life.

2. Eat mindfully: Pay attention to your diet. Nutritious meals can significantly impact your energy levels and mood. Eating regular, balanced meals can maintain or improve your physical health, which is often neglected during times of emotional stress.

3. Create a safe and comfortable space: Make your living environment a sanctuary. This could mean decluttering, adding elements that bring you joy, or simply organizing your space in a way that makes you feel comfortable and more relaxed.

4. Get quality sleep: Prioritize good sleep hygiene. A consistent sleep schedule and a comfortable sleeping environment are essential for mental and physical recovery.

5. Use mindfulness and relaxation techniques: Practices like meditation, deep breathing exercises, or yoga are great techniques for calming the mind and reducing stress. They can be powerful tools for regaining emotional balance.

6. Pursue hobbies and interests: Reengage with activities and hobbies you enjoy. Reading, painting, hiking, or any other interest you have can distract you from negative thoughts and be a source of joy, fulfillment, and pride.

7. Regaining emotional and physical stability after partner betrayal is a gradual process. It requires patience, self-compassion, and often a reevaluation of your daily life and habits. By focusing on these practical steps, you can start to bring back a sense of order and security to your life, paving the way for deeper healing and recovery. Each small action toward stability is a step forward in reclaiming control over your life and well-being.

UNDERSTANDING AND MANAGING TRIGGERS

Following betrayal, your emotional landscape goes through some reorganization. Triggers erupt unexpectedly and surprisingly like landmines. Your reactions can be intense. As remotely and unconnected as they might appear, they are often directly linked to the experience of your betrayal. They can be diverse and come at you sideways—catching you off guard. Don't think they can't significantly impact your emotional well-being.

Triggers in the context of betrayal trauma can manifest in various forms:

- Memorable locations: Places that you and your partner frequented or that hold special memories can act as potent triggers. Visiting or passing by these locations can evoke strong emotional responses.

- Significant dates: Dates that once held positive significance, such as anniversaries, birthdays, or other milestones, can turn into painful reminders of what was lost or betrayed.

- Music and media: Songs, movies, or even certain TV shows that you associate with your partner or relationship can trigger memories and feelings related to the betrayal or feelings of what you are now missing.

- Shared phrases or inside jokes: Words or phrases that were unique or special to your relationship can trigger emotional responses when heard or recalled.

- Scents and sensory reminders: Sometimes, even specific scents or sensory experiences linked to your partner or significant events in your relationship can act as triggers.

- Social media and photos: Encountering your partner on social media or coming across photos and digital reminders of your time together can be triggering.

THE IMPACT OF TRIGGERS

Triggers act as conduits, transporting you back to the moments of pain and betrayal, often with an intensity that can be surprising and overwhelming. The experience can be surprisingly vivid and fresh, like reliving the pain and shock as if it were happening right now. Painful reminders can disrupt your entire day or longer, affecting your mood and potentially even derailing or delaying your progress in healing.

Triggers aren't just fleeting moments of discomfort; they can greatly impact your daily life. An example of this is avoidance behaviors, when you may be tempted to steer clear of places, people, or activities you once enjoyed. Triggers can also manifest physically with symptoms like increased heart rate, anxiety, or even panic attacks. Emotionally, they can contribute to feelings of sadness, anger, or a sense of loss.

Triggers are a normal part of the healing process. You must understand they are necessary—as painful and unwanted as they are important. They are indicators of the deep emotional impact of betrayal and signify areas where you still have work to do in emotional processing and healing. Learning to navigate these triggers effectively is a vital step in your journey toward recovery and emotional stability.

PRACTICAL ADVICE

1. Recognize and acknowledge triggers: The first step in managing triggers is recognizing and acknowledging them. Pay attention to the moments when your emotions seem to intensify suddenly. What just happened? What did you see, hear, or think about?

2. Journal for awareness: Keep a journal to keep track of your triggers. Note the circumstances when a trigger occurs, the time, place, and people involved, and how you felt. This can help you identify patterns and prepare for potential triggers. When you are prepared for a trigger, it does take some of the sting out of the experience.

3. Develop avoidance strategies: If certain places or situations consistently trigger you, consider avoiding them for a while. This doesn't have to be a permanent change, but giving yourself some distance can be beneficial in the initial stages of healing.

4. Create a response plan: For unavoidable triggers, develop a plan for how you'll respond. This could involve breathing exercises, stepping away from the situation for a moment, or having a supportive person to call.

5. Reframe triggers: Therapy or self-guided exercises can help you reframe your perception of triggers or become desensitized to them. This involves changing how you interpret and react to them, reducing their emotional impact over time.

6. Practice mindfulness: Engage in mindfulness practices. Being mindful helps in staying grounded in the present moment, making it easier to navigate through the sudden wave of emotions brought on by triggers.

7. Seek professional help: If you find it challenging to manage your triggers, consider seeking support from a mental health professional. They can provide strategies and tools to cope with and diminish the power of these triggers.

8. Build a support network: Share your experience with trusted friends or support groups. Sometimes, just talking about what triggers you can lessen its impact.

9.   Engage in self-care routines: Self-care routines can bolster your emotional resilience, such as physical exercise, hobbies, favorite pastimes, relaxation techniques, a massage session, or a spa day—activities that help maintain a relaxed, balanced emotional state.

10. Develop positive affirmations: A set of positive affirmations or mantras that you repeat to yourself can be useful when a trigger occurs. You can also say them in front of a mirror as you prepare your morning routines or while you're in bed getting ready for sleep. They can remind you of your strength, journey, and ability to overcome challenges.

While triggers can be challenging, they are also opportunities for growth and healing. Each time you successfully diffuse a trigger, you reinforce your resilience and move one step closer to healing. Over time, as you continue to work through your emotions and understand your triggers, their power over you will diminish, allowing you to regain more and more control over your emotional well-being.

THE CRUCIAL ROLE OF BOUNDARIES IN RECOVERY

Establishing boundaries after experiencing betrayal significantly accelerates the healing process and your ability to reclaim your sense of self. Betrayal can leave you feeling exposed and vulnerable as your sense of trust and safety is shattered. Boundaries act as gateposts that help define your limits and terms during interactions and emotional exchanges. They serve as protective barriers, allowing you to regain a sense of control and power in a situation where you might feel uncertain or uncomfortable.

KEY TYPES OF BOUNDARIES

Establishing boundaries after betrayal can encompass various aspects of your life:

- Emotional boundaries: These involve managing the level and depth of emotional engagement, especially concerning conversations about the betrayal.

- Physical boundaries: This might mean setting limits on physical contact, including decisions about intimacy and personal space.

- Digital boundaries: Because we live in a digital age, it's important to set boundaries around online interactions, including social media and other digital communications.

ENFORCING BOUNDARIES: PRACTICAL STEPS

1.   Communication: Clearly articulate your boundaries to those involved. Be assertive yet respectful to ensure your needs are understood.

2.   Consistency: Consistently uphold your boundaries. This reinforces their importance to both yourself and others.

3.   Flexibility: Allow your boundaries to evolve as your healing progresses. What you need immediately post-betrayal may change over time.

Establishing and maintaining boundaries isn't all about protection, and it's not a fear-based posture. It's an aspect of self-care and emotional well-being. As you navigate your recovery, your boundaries will provide a framework for rebuilding trust and respect in both your current relationships and future interactions. In the next chapter, I'll examine the process of establishing and maintaining these boundaries, exploring how they can support your healing and empowerment.

WHO TO TELL

After experiencing the pain of partner betrayal, one of the critical decisions you will face is choosing with whom to share this experience. The decision is delicate and multi-faceted, balancing your need for support and empathy with your desire to maintain privacy and discretion. The choice of who to confide in can significantly impact your healing journey and the dynamics of your existing relationship with the betrayer.

PRACTICAL ADVICE

1. Evaluate the trustworthiness of potential confidants: Before sharing, assess a person's trustworthiness. Have they been supportive and understanding in the past? Do they keep confidence? Choosing people who will respect your privacy and the sensitivity of the information is vital.

2. Consider the benefits of professional confidentiality: Professional counselors or therapists are bound by confidentiality and can provide a safe space to share your feelings without the risk of judgment or unwanted gossip.

3.   Share selectively: You don't have to share every detail. Decide what you're comfortable sharing. Some details may be too personal or painful to discuss, and that's okay.

4.   Reflect on the purpose of sharing: Consider what you hope to achieve by sharing your experience. Are you seeking advice, empathy, or simply a listening ear? Understanding your objectives can help you choose the right person to confide in and what you say.

5.   Prepare for mixed reactions: Be prepared for a range of reactions. Some might offer support or show anger toward your situation, while others may feel uncomfortable or stay quiet, not understanding the depth of your experience. Bracing yourself for responses that may not align with your expectations is important.

6.   Limit the circle of disclosure: While sharing your pain with many might be tempting, limiting the circle of people who know can help maintain a sense of control over and sensitivity to your story.

7.   Gauge the impact on relationships: Consider how sharing this information might impact your relationships with mutual friends or family members.

Think about the potential consequences of these relationships for you and your partner.

8. Respect your partner's privacy: While you have the right to seek support, be mindful of your partner's privacy. Avoid sharing details that could unnecessarily harm their reputation or exacerbate the situation.

Remember, the decision of who to tell about the betrayal is intensely personal and varies from one individual to another. It's not just a matter of who you tell but also how much you choose to share, how, and when. This process is about finding the right balance between seeking the support you need and protecting your boundaries. It requires careful consideration and often a bit of introspection to understand what will best serve your healing process.

Trust your instincts in this situation, as they often guide you toward individuals who will understand and provide the support you require. Take into account the consequences of sharing your story, weigh them against your emotional needs, and consider how it may impact your future well-being. Remember, opening up about your experience of betrayal doesn't mean giving up control over your story or healing journey.

Be prepared to reassess your decisions as you continue your healing journey. The people who can offer support may change over time. Your comfort level in discussing what happened may evolve as well. It's perfectly alright to adjust how much information you disclose as you progress forward. Above all, remember that seeking support is a courageous step in your path to healing. Whether you choose to confide in a close friend, professional counselor, or support group, you are taking an important step toward processing your emotions and regaining your sense of self. Each conversation can work toward closure and recovery, helping you navigate through this challenging time in a way that fosters resilience and personal growth.

FINDING THE PATH TO HEALING

As this chapter concludes, think of the journey through betrayal trauma as a path marked by challenges and an avenue leading toward profound growth and healing. The tools and insights provided in this chapter are designed to help you manage the immediate and often overwhelming crisis that betrayal can bring into your life.

As you move forward, hold onto the promise of healing and the potential for transformation that lies within you.

Your path to recovery is deeply personal and unique, but it is also paved with hope and resilience. With each step, you are moving away from the pain of betrayal and toward a future of greater understanding, strength, and emotional well-being. Remember, amid adversity lies the opportunity for personal growth and renewal.

MY EXPERIENCE

I must admit I didn't handle the aftermath of my then-wife's betrayal well at all in the beginning. I was stuck in a state of shock for what seemed like an eternity, wrestling with sleepless nights and panic attacks that would jolt me awake. The weight of fear, shame, and overwhelming loneliness consumed me, and for a time I felt utterly directionless, not knowing where to turn for support. I even got a kidney stone a few months after discovery of the affair, which was no surprise based on the trauma my body was processing.

My relationship with my then-wife morphed in a way I never anticipated, transforming her from a life partner to someone who seemed to hold the reins to my future—a business partner or, in some ways, almost a boss—roles I never wanted or asked for but allowed to happen, and in many cases, helped create myself. This shift created a feeling of powerlessness where I was lost without the tools to manage the torrent of emotions I faced daily. The world around me felt like a minefield of triggers: love songs on the radio, romantic plots on TV, and seemingly happy couples everywhere I went served as constant reminders of what I had lost, deepening my isolation.

Couples therapy offered a glimmer of hope, but it was fleeting. The ambivalence from my then-wife to work on reconciling and respecting my boundaries and the overall complexities of our lives cut that path short. I found myself yearning to do the work necessary to heal, yet I was clueless about what that entailed, where to find help, or how to begin. Resources online were limited, and no books were geared for what a man might be experiencing.

My saving grace came in the form of my men's group. The men, or shall I call them my band of brothers, offered me a sanctuary—a space free from judgment where I could voice my feelings over and over, confront my anger and grief, and start the process of healing. This experience taught me a key lesson: Navigating the aftermath of betrayal wasn't a journey I could or should undertake alone. Despite my initial reluctance to seek help, the support and understanding I found in my men's group were instrumental in moving me from a place of being stuck to one of gradual healing and self-discovery.

Chapter 3:

SETTING BOUNDARIES AFTER BETRAYAL

Partner betrayal is a gut punch that leaves you questioning everything, including yourself. In the aftermath of my partner's betrayal, it felt more than a breach of trust; it was like the world had crumbled around me. Suddenly, I was caught in a whirlwind of emotions, unsure what to do next. It was a period of isolation, where even the comforts of silence only seemed to amplify my pain.

In this space of despair, I realized that I longed for guidance, a roadmap for the path ahead. The concept of boundaries became invaluable, like lifelines holding me together. Through my expertise and encounters, I have come to understand how important boundaries are in the process of healing from partner betrayal, empowering you to reclaim your sense of self and establish a framework for moving forward.

CRAFTING AND COMMUNICATING BOUNDARIES

Crafting and effectively communicating boundaries is paramount after being blindsided by betrayal because it allows you to create a map to lead you through tough terrain. Expressing what you need helps you regain a sense of security and emotional well-being.

Let's explore how you can establish boundaries and effectively adhere to them.

- Communicate clearly: Your boundaries clarify your voice. They articulate your needs, limits, and expectations for moving forward. You're saying, "This is what I need to feel safe and respected."

- Stay on track: Consistency is key. Your boundaries aren't up for negotiation. They're the pillars that uphold your healing journey, ensuring that your path to recovery is built on a foundation of respect and understanding.

- You first: Setting boundaries is an act of self-respect. It's a declaration that you value your well-being and are committed to protecting your emotional and psychological space.

- Be adaptable: Healing is a dynamic process. As you grow and heal, your boundaries may shift. Stay open to this evolution, allowing them to reflect where you are at a given point in time.

WHEN IT GETS TOUGH

Establishing boundaries can be challenging at times, especially if the other person doesn't immediately understand or is in their own stuck place. Here are a few strategies to keep in mind:

- Expect some pushback: Not everyone is going to be on board right away. Be ready for a bit of resistance and have a game plan for dealing with it.

- Self-care is key: This whole boundary thing can be draining. Make sure you're taking care of your heart, head, and body.

- Learn as you go: The more you know about what boundaries really mean, the better you'll be at setting yours. The term "boundaries" gets tossed around a lot. Hit the books or the internet and get clued in on identifying and putting them into practice.

- Stand your ground: Practice being assertive. It's not about being bossy; it's about respecting your needs.

- Check-in with yourself: Now and then, take a moment to see if your boundaries are still doing their job. If not, it's tweak time.

If you're struggling with establishing and maintaining boundaries, seek guidance from a professional like a therapist or betrayal trauma coach. Setting boundaries is about reclaiming control and ensuring you're treated with the respect and dignity you deserve. It's a step toward rediscovering yourself and moving forward from the past hurt.

NON-NEGOTIABLE BOUNDARIES

Setting non-negotiable boundaries involves setting limits regarding behaviors or actions that you cannot and will not tolerate. These boundaries are critical in establishing a sense of safety and respect with others— particularly with those close to you. Examples of non-negotiable boundaries might include for your partner:

- Zero tolerance for sexual misconduct: Any form of sexual activity outside your relationship, including physical encounters or virtual interactions, is unacceptable.

- Honesty and transparency: Complete honesty is always required. This includes no lying, gaslighting, or evasive behavior that obscures the truth.

- Appropriate use of digital content: Don't engage with pornographic material, including viewing, possessing, or distributing such content.

- Respectful interactions: All interactions with others—whether in person or online—should be respectful and appropriate. Avoid any form of flirting or suggestive behavior.

- Avoid unhealthy behavior triggers: Steer clear of any online content or television shows that may reinforce or trigger unhealthy habits or patterns.

- Steer clear of dating and chat platforms: Don't use dating websites, apps, or chat rooms for romantic or sexual purposes.

- Cut ties with past inappropriate connections: Sever all contact with individuals previously associated with acting-out behaviors, including blocking and deleting them from all platforms.

- Commit to therapy and recovery programs: Attend and participate regularly in therapy, betrayal coaching sessions, or twelve-step meetings. These programs should be considered mandatory for your continued growth and recovery.

- Accountability measures: Install accountability software on all your personal devices. Keep passwords to those sites current and share them with your partner.

- Using devices transparently: Be open and transparent in your use of phones, computers, and other devices to those in your support group. This includes no secretive behavior like hiding or deleting history, contacts, or data.

- Proactively disclose lapses: Any lapses or slips in behavior should be disclosed within 24 hours to maintain transparency and trust.

- Avoid replacing unhealthy behaviors: Be on the lookout for and refrain from substituting one behavior problem (such as infidelity or pornography) with another (like excessive video gaming or overeating).

- Actively engage in self-improvement: Demonstrate you are genuinely committed to your growth, including attending therapy and engaging in regular self-reflection and check-ins.

If boundaries are crossed, you might consider various responses to protect yourself and ensure that the seriousness of the violation is understood. You might get back on track more quickly, keep from escalating a situation by requesting more therapy, or consider pausing or ending a relationship.

PHYSICAL BOUNDARIES

Physical boundaries are necessary for reestablishing a sense of personal space and comfort. They can include:

- Initiating physical contact: You have the right to decide when and how you want to be touched. This boundary is about respecting your space and doing what makes you feel comfortable.

- Leading physical intimacy: Make decisions about when it feels right to engage in any form of intimacy or sexual activity. Be emotionally and physically comfortable with the progression of intimacy.

- Respect personal time and activities: If you're involved in something or working on a task, let your partner know that you appreciate them giving you space until you're ready to engage in conversation or other interactions.

- Timing of significant conversations: Reserve discussions on sensitive topics for times when you and your partner are both mentally prepared and not overwhelmed with work or other stresses. Agree on a time after work when you are both available to have uninterrupted and undistracted conversations with the attention and sensitivity they deserve.

If you violate your limits, you could request space. Space examples might be dressing privately or sleeping in separate rooms.

SEXUAL BOUNDARIES

Sexual boundaries are important for redefining the sexual aspect of your relationship post-betrayal. These boundaries help in creating a safe space for sexual expression and might include:

- Initiating sexual activity: As mentioned above, you have the right to maintain and initiate any sexual activity or play to ensure you feel completely comfortable and give your consent to any progression in your intimacy. Your readiness and willingness will guide your interactions.

- Restrictions on inappropriate behavior: No suggestive comments, physical grabbing of your body, making sexual jokes, or implying any form of sexual activity without agreeing mutually. This boundary is set to uphold a safe environment where your expressions of sexuality are mutually agreeable and considerate of each other's boundaries.

If these established sexual boundaries are crossed, take appropriate measures to safeguard your well-being and reinforce your boundaries. This may involve:

- Communicating clearly and demanding a halt to any inappropriate behavior.

- Creating distance to reestablish a sense of comfort and respect for boundaries.

- Reiterating the importance of these boundaries and the need to strictly adhere to them to maintain a healthy and respectful sexual relationship.

Boundaries are not intended to punish; rather, they create a consensual space for your physical interactions. They play a role in ensuring that you feel safe and comfortable while also fostering a relationship where both partners feel respected and valued in their expressions of sexuality.

EMOTIONAL BOUNDARIES

Emotional boundaries help manage the emotional aspects of your relationship. These might involve:

- Seeking appropriate support: The betrayer should seek support for their addiction or infidelity issues from professionals such as therapists, accountability partners, or members of a 12-step group. It's best to be cautious around seeking support from your family or friends as this can blur the lines between recovery and dynamics within your relationship.

- Allowing space during triggering moments: If you're emotionally triggered, kindly request that the betraying partner give you the necessary space and time to process those feelings. Refrain from becoming defensive or angry or attempting to minimize your emotions during these moments. Respecting your space is essential for your healing.

- Communicating honestly: Honesty is necessary— no compromises. Ask your partner to be honest with you. Ask them to give you the level of detail you need when discussing issues related to the betrayal. You both need to be transparent to rebuild trust.

- Healing through collaboration: You might strongly encourage the betraying partner to work with their therapist to identify actions that can help you both regain a sense of safety and security in your relationship. Collaborating on this journey is important. It shows your commitment to repairing the harm caused.

- Being accountable when apart: When one of you is away from home, talk about steps the betraying partner can take to maintain accountability. Let them know this helps ensure there are no inappropriate behaviors and reassures you of their dedication to your healing. Proactively communicating about their whereabouts and activities greatly contributes to rebuilding trust and provides peace of mind.

If these emotional boundaries are not respected, you need to take measures to safeguard your well-being. These may include:

- Request a pause in your conversation or interaction until you feel ready to reengage.

- Seek a support network or therapist to process your feelings independently.

- Reiterate the need for honest and open communication, and if necessary, involve a couple's therapist to facilitate this.

- Evaluate the steps needed to feel safe in the relationship, which may involve physically distancing yourself temporarily or reevaluating your relationship status.

These boundaries protect your emotional well-being and lay the groundwork for a healthier, more honest relationship dynamic. They are significant in navigating the complex emotions following betrayal and are integral to the healing process for both partners.

ADDITIONAL BOUNDARIES

- Blocking inappropriate content: To maintain a home environment that supports your relationship's recovery, kindly request installing filtering software to block access to pornography, written erotica, and any other inappropriate websites or apps. Agree to limit computer and phone use to certain areas of your house. While this step might seem harsh and may imply your lack of trust in them, in the long term, it promotes transparency, avoids exposure to content that could hinder your progress, and is a reflection of your partner's sincere desire to support the relationship and your healing journey.

- Cutting ties with negative influences: Cut off contact with individuals who have been involved in or supported the behaviors that contributed to the betrayal. This includes ending relationships with anyone complicit or supportive of these actions. Distancing from these associations demonstrates their commitment to change and reduces the risk of falling into destructive patterns.

If any of these boundaries are crossed, agree to take measures to safeguard the integrity of your home and relationship. This may involve:

- Reinforcing the importance of these boundaries and discussing the consequences of violating them

- Reassessing your living arrangements to ensure your need for a respectful home environment is met

- Seeking support or counseling to address any challenges in upholding these boundaries

Again, let me stress that these boundaries should not be set up to punish but rather to create a nurturing environment for both of you, which will impact the healing of your relationship. They help to return trust and respect, which are fundamental aspects of moving forward after betrayal.

THE POWER OF BOUNDARIES

Establishing boundaries following betrayal is also not a protective measure. It's an act of self-empowerment and an expression of your needs and values. These boundaries serve as indicators of what you're willing to accept and what you're not while providing an environment conducive to healing. They are tools you can use to regain control and ensure safety within your relationship.

By setting these boundaries, you actively commit to healing. It's not so easy. This process requires courage and self-awareness because you will need to figure out what makes you feel safe and how to communicate those needs to your partner. Boundaries create a new normal for your relationship—one based on respect, trust, and understanding.

MY EXPERIENCE

Reflecting on my journey, I now see how daunting setting boundaries is in the aftermath of partner betrayal. Just days after my then-wife confessed her affair, I was thrust into an emotional storm, uncertain of what I needed to feel secure again. My initial attempts at setting boundaries were feeble and ill-defined—more out of fear of further loss than taking a stand for my well-being. I was terrified of pushing her away with strong boundaries, fearing they might be the death blow that ends our marriage—a marriage I was desperately clinging to despite her actions. I also didn't seek personal professional help or support, having no real idea how to manage my needs or what was appropriate or not.

In a bid to hold onto the remnants of what we had, I let her dictate the terms of our going forward, even when it meant that she would continue her contact with the person she had the affair with. In many ways, I felt like I didn't have a choice, which I now know wasn't true. I hoped to save us and return to a semblance of normality, which blinded me to the reality that our relationship as I knew it was in many ways beyond salvageable. I compromised on boundaries that should have been non-negotiable, allowing her unchecked interactions and time with her affair partner—convincing myself that it was a necessary sacrifice to mend our bond.

As time wore on and the promised check-ins and assurances dwindled, I remained silent and stuck in my fear, my voice lost in the chaos of my internal conflict when deep down I knew it was over. This concession only served to perpetuate the cycle of betrayal, effectively keeping the door open for their relationship to continue, albeit under a different guise. It became increasingly clear that without solid, respected boundaries, the path to healing and reconciliation was obstructed, if not entirely blocked. My experience taught me the hard lesson that boundaries are the foundation on which trust can begin to be rebuilt, and without them, we stand on shaky ground.

Chapter 4:

THE MALE EGO

Let's dive deep into an aspect of your identity whose impact you might not fully grasp, especially when partner betrayal hits home: your ego. The ego is more encompassing than just being arrogant or self-assured. It's deeply intertwined with your self-perception, your self-worth, and how you evaluate yourself within your life. Society has its own expectations for what it means to be a man, influencing everything from how you handle success to navigating through your darkest moments.

In Ryan Holiday's book, *Ego is the Enemy*, the author portrays the ego as a voice that often leads you astray from reality:

> The ego is the enemy, giving us wicked feedback, disconnected from reality. It's defensive, precisely when we cannot afford to be defensive. It blocks us from improving by telling us we don't need to improve. Then we wonder why we don't get the results we want, why others are better, and why their success is more lasting (42).

As a result, you wonder why you fail to achieve desired results, why others outperform you, and why their success endures longer. This insight emphasizes how the ego impedes your growth and objective self-reflection.

It's often challenging to admit when you're hurt or in need of help. Most of us have been raised with the belief that we must always be strong. This mindset can leave you trapped, denying your feelings and struggling alone—making healing from partner betrayal even harder. Your ego suffers a blow when infidelity disrupts your life, causing you to question your value and your role as a man.

Discussing the ego in the context of betrayal is like unraveling a puzzle where each piece reflects how you perceive yourself, your worthiness, and your position in the world. When infidelity shatters this reflection, it deeply affects your ego and makes you feel let down. Beyond feeling betrayed, it's also about grappling with the thought that maybe you are not enough. This sting goes deep, stirring up a mix of anger, pain, and a sense of loss that can be challenging to navigate.

Here's the thing: Understanding and working through your ego isn't about tamping down these feelings or pretending they don't exist. It's about getting real with yourself, acknowledging the ego's grip on your self-image, and figuring out how to move from anger and hurt toward healing and growth.

Navigating the ego involves examining how you assess your self-worth and achievements. It entails challenging the expectations that define vulnerability as a weakness. During my betrayal period, I experienced the struggle of reconciling the image I believed I should portray with the reality of myself. It is a tough journey that presents an opportunity to rediscover your inner resilience—not the kind that gains societal approval but rather the resilience that emerges from confronting your truths, embracing your emotions, and seeking support when needed.

The role of your ego in navigating partner betrayal extends beyond a backdrop. It is central to your healing process and significantly influences how you interpret and handle everything that transpires and shapes the path you choose for recovery. By understanding and guiding your ego through this process, you're redefining your sense of self, your values, and how you relate to the world.

THE EGO'S RESPONSE TO PARTNER BETRAYAL

When confronted with the reality of a partner's infidelity, the male ego often experiences a shock that strikes at the core of its identity and perception of its role in society. It triggers a series of questions that challenge one's sense of self-worth and understanding of masculinity—questions like, "Was I not enough?" or

"How did I miss the signs?" or "Am I lacking as a man?" These are reflexive inquiries, arising as the ego seeks to comprehend this newfound pain.

In an attempt to protect itself from this turmoil, the ego may resort to various defense mechanisms. These can include:

- Denial: Refusing to accept the reality of the situation, often as a means of self-preservation to avoid confronting the associated pain

- Anger: A visceral response serving as a mask for deeper feelings of hurt, betrayal, and vulnerability

- Control: An intensified need for regaining control over one's life or relationships, often to counteract feelings of helplessness or chaos

PRACTICAL ADVICE

1. Acknowledge your emotions: Recognize and accept what you're feeling. It's normal to feel anger, want to deny what has happened, or take charge of the situation. These reactions are initial natural urges when faced with betrayal.

2. Seek outlets: Look for ways to manage your anger and confusion without letting them consume you.

Engage in activities like going to the gym, expressing yourself through art or a favorite hobby, or venting by screaming into a pillow. Find what helps you release tension in a positive, non-destructive way.

3. Confront denial: If you're pretending that everything is fine when it's not, it may be time to challenge those thoughts and confront your feelings. Consider talking with a trusted friend, journaling your emotions, or seeking guidance as steps toward healing.

4. Embrace mindfulness: Mindfulness is more than a fashionable term. It's a valuable tool for self-discovery by helping you recognize how your ego influences your thoughts and steers you toward interpreting your emotions with clarity.

5. Professional support: Sometimes people require the expertise of professionals who can guide them through difficult times. Therapists and wellness coaches have strategies to help you understand and navigate your emotions, guiding you toward an escape route rather than toward an ego trap.

6. Practice self-compassion: Healing takes time. Be kind to yourself, allowing space for growth and self-reflection along the way.

7. Redefine your self-perception: Remind yourself that you are more than the recipient of a betrayal. You're not defined by someone else's actions or by outdated ideas of masculinity.

8. Communication: If you and your partner are working through things, find a safe space to express how you're feeling. This might mean having tough conversations, ideally with a professional's help.

9. Embrace vulnerability: Allowing yourself to let go of your defenses may be intimidating but necessary for healing. You are being true to yourself in the most authentic way possible.

10. Seek support networks: You are not alone in this journey. Connecting with others who empathize with your experiences can be comforting and provide perspectives and emotional support that help you feel better and motivate you to make positive changes.

STUCK IN THE EGO TRAP

By recognizing and managing the ego's reaction to partner betrayal, you can better navigate your journey following infidelity. Understanding your reactions and finding better ways to address them is essential for healing and moving forward.

The ego trap can be deceptive—it's what the ego is very good at. It tricks you into downplaying the depth of your betrayal. Yes, it can minimize your pain and soften the emotional effects, but it will also masquerade, deflect, or rationalize the situation. The ego can trick you into sublimating that pain rather than exposing it to heal like a physical wound that needs air. Getting angry is often a reaction that masks your vulnerabilities and becomes a distraction from addressing your real emotions. When you build a wall of self-protection, you're isolating yourself further and cutting off the support that could aid in your healing process. It's commonly known as the "trap," and it can manifest in the following ways:

- Denial and minimization: The ego may push you to deny the impact of the betrayal, minimize it, or rationalize it away. This is a defense mechanism to avoid fully confronting the painful emotions tied to the betrayal.

- Anger and blame: The ego might direct the pain outward, leading to physical expressions of anger, blame, and sometimes revenge. While these are natural responses, they are often the ego's way of diverting attention from internal pain and vulnerability.

- Inflated self-protection: In an attempt to safeguard itself, the ego may inflate itself, leading to a heightened sense of pride and a refusal to seek help or admit the need for support.

Breaking free from the ego's trap is necessary to move forward. It all begins with acknowledging these defense mechanisms for what they truly are: responses to the deep-seated pain of betrayal. This realization doesn't mean you are weak. You are discovering strength in your vulnerability while recognizing that your worth is not defined by others' actions. Embarking on a journey of self-discovery and growth will reshape your sense of self in a more genuine and balanced way.

EGO AND SELF-WORTH

Then, there's the link between your ego and your self-worth. It's like a double blow to your trust and how you see yourself. You start questioning everything—your attractiveness, your abilities, and even your self-worth as an individual. This self-doubt can spiral, leading you to withdraw, perform poorly at work, or shy away from new relationships. It's a cycle where your ego tries to protect you, and in the process, it might amplify your feelings of inadequacy.

The key lies in taking a step back and recognizing that your worth is separate from the actions of your partner and social expectations. It involves embracing a non-traditional perspective on masculinity that celebrates vulnerability and emotional openness as strengths rather than weaknesses. Rebuilding your self-worth means leaning on others, finding joy in activities that affirm who you are, and, if necessary, seeking professional help. On this path, you can grow into a more self-assured, compassionate man.

PRACTICAL ADVICE

1. Recognize your strengths: Take some time to reflect on your good qualities and accomplishments. Jot them down. Remind yourself of the strengths you possess regardless of others' actions.

2. Challenge negative thoughts: When you find yourself spiraling down the self-doubt drain, put in the stopper. Hit the pause button. Question those thoughts. Are they true? Are they simply your ego's way of shielding you from pain? Once you've

identified where they're coming from, replace them with affirmations and truths about yourself.

3. Embrace vulnerability: Sharing your emotions is a step toward healing, not a sign of weakness. Whether you confide in trusted friends or family members or join a support group, opening up about your experiences can lighten the load and remind you you're not alone.

4. Finding joy: Whether it's exercising, pursuing hobbies, or learning something new, doing things that make you happy cannot help but uplift your mood and boost your confidence. You are reconnecting with yourself and rediscovering or newly discovering what brings you joy.

5. Set small, achievable goals: Accomplishing tasks, regardless of their size, can give you a sense of fulfillment and rebuild your confidence. Establish goals for yourself in both your professional and personal life, and when you achieve them, take the time to celebrate.

6. Practice self-compassion: Be gentle with yourself. Recovering from betrayal takes time, and there are lapses along the way. It's perfectly normal to have good days as well as bad ones. Treat yourself with

the kindness and understanding you would extend to a friend going through a situation.

7.   Reconnect with your values: Betrayal can sometimes provoke you to question many things you believe in. Take it as an opportunity to reflect on what matters to you. What values define who you are? Why not adopt values that make more sense now? Aligning your life with these newfound principles can help restore your sense of self-worth.

8.   Limit comparison: Avoid comparing your journey to others. Everyone's path to healing is unique. Focus on your progress, not where others seem to be.

9.   Future vision: Betrayal can shatter the present, but it doesn't have to define your future. Imagine the life you want to lead and the person you want to be. Start taking small steps toward that vision.

MOVING BEYOND THE EGO

Moving beyond your ego after partner betrayal is a journey of introspection, support-seeking, and resilience-building. It doesn't mean restoring everything that once was and that you once felt. It's about challenging your perceptions, stripping out what's not working anymore, embracing your vulnerability, and finding strength in your true self. Through this process, you learn that healing and growth are within your grasp. You can rediscover your worth and transform your pain into a powerful force for personal change.

MY EXPERIENCE

Reflecting on my ego journey through partner betrayal, I realize now how deeply my ego was entangled in the entire process. That moment at the kitchen table when my world shattered with the revelation of my then-wife's affair was just the beginning of a long and tumultuous path. My immediate thoughts of "How do I fix this?" and "What is my part?" was my ego's way of stepping in and trying to maintain control over a situation that felt utterly chaotic and unbearable.

In the wake of the betrayal, I found myself oscillating between intense pain and a determined resolve to mend what had been broken. It was a stark illustration of how the ego can simultaneously act as both a shield and a cage. It sought to protect me from the full impact of the pain, offering up denial and a narrative that maybe—just maybe—things could return to how they once were if I just tried hard enough. It trapped me in a cycle of self-blame and an almost desperate need to "win" back the love and trust that had been so callously disregarded. My denial clouded my reality, inadvertently absolving her of a lot of the responsibility for her actions. I struggled to understand how, on one hand, I could love this person who caused me so much pain and, at the same time, want them to fix and console me for the very pain they were responsible for creating. This feeling was truly a deep space of dissidence.

My internal battle was a clear embodiment of the "ego trap" I've come to understand so well. My ego was in full swing, employing denial and minimization to spare me from facing the harsh truth of my situation. Yet, this very mechanism also kept me from acknowledging the depth of my hurt and vulnerability, from truly processing my emotions and moving toward healing.

My experience highlights the intricate dance between ego and self-worth in the aftermath of betrayal. It underscores the importance of navigating your ego wisely, recognizing its protective mechanisms while also challenging its limitations. Doing so allows you to move beyond the immediate pain and embark on a path of true healing and personal evolution. This journey isn't just about overcoming the betrayal. It's about redefining your sense of self and emerging from the experience stronger, more self-aware, and more resilient than ever before.

Chapter 5:

THE SEVEN STAGES
OF NAVIGATING BETRAYAL

UNDERSTANDING THE MBT RECOVERY™ MODEL

The MBT Recovery™ Model (Masculine Betrayal Trauma) helps you navigate the aftermath of your partner's infidelity. It provides a framework to understand and process your emotions and reactions triggered by betrayal. Recognizing where you stand in this journey is essential for several reasons.

Validates feelings: Understanding the stages of MBT Recovery™ helps you realize that your emotional responses are normal and expected. In a world where men are often discouraged from openly expressing vulnerability or hurt, knowing that your feelings are real, valid, and worthy of acknowledgment—regardless of what society wants you to believe—can be both freeing and healing.

Guides emotional processing: By identifying which stage of MBT Recovery™ you're experiencing, you can better focus on relevant coping strategies and emotional work. Each stage requires a different approach to healing. Understanding this helps you adapt the recovery process to your specific needs.

Brings self-awareness and insight: The MBT Recovery™ model encourages you to develop deeper self-awareness. With this insight, you will understand your responses to betrayal, including how your ego and self-worth are impacted, leading to more clarity and acceptance.

Helps with navigating your healing journey: Knowing your stage in the MBT Recovery™ model means you can follow a roadmap on your healing journey. It helps you set realistic expectations and recognize that healing from betrayal is a process that evolves over time.

Empowers through knowledge: Understanding the MBT Recovery™ model empowers you with knowledge. This understanding allows you to take active steps in your healing rather than feeling helpless in the face of your emotions.

Facilitates support and communication: Recognizing your stage in the MBT Recovery™ model can also help you communicate your needs and challenges more easily to therapists, counselors, and support networks. It becomes a language to articulate your experiences more clearly.

WHY MBT RECOVERY™ IS IMPORTANT

MBT Recovery™ addresses how men experience and navigate betrayal trauma differently than women. Society's expectations of masculinity can greatly influence how a man responds to infidelity. It's a perspective that considers the role of societal pressures and the emotional complexities specific to you.

Following this model guides you through emotional turmoil and provides a framework for redefining and understanding your masculinity within the context of emotional trauma. It encourages you to explore and redefine your notions of strength, vulnerability, and self-worth. Redefining yourself is necessary for moving beyond traditional stereotypes and embracing a more holistic, authentic sense of yourself.

Using MBT Recovery™ as a tool to understand and navigate your journey, you can find clarity, validation, and a path toward recovery that acknowledges the challenges you face in difficult situations. You can take important steps that bring you closer to healing and personal growth. There is a way out of the painful event of partner betrayal, and you are capable of becoming that more resilient and self-aware man.

DIAGRAM OF THE SEVEN STAGES OF MBT RECOVERY™

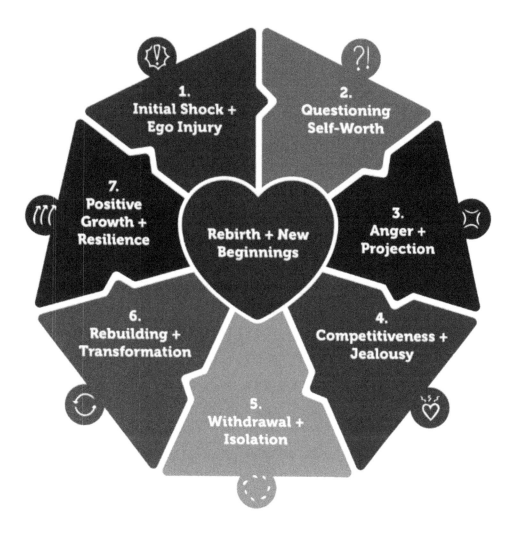

THE SEVEN STAGES OF MBT RECOVERY™:

1. Initial shock and ego injury: The first stage is marked by a profound shock to your ego, leading to feelings of humiliation and inadequacy.

2. Questioning self-worth: At this stage, intense self-reflection and doubt surface, leading to questions about your desirability and value as a partner.

3. Anger and projection: A common response is projection, where anger is directed outwardly as a defense mechanism, often accompanied by blaming your partner or the person with whom they were unfaithful.

4. Competitiveness and jealousy: You may experience a heightened sense of rivalry, driven by a need to restore your pride and counteract feelings of inadequacy.

5. Withdrawal and isolation: You may have a tendency to withdraw socially to avoid discussing the betrayal for fear of being judged or seen as a failure.

6. Rebuilding and transformation: This stage involves significantly reevaluating your personal values and beliefs about relationships, leading to making changes about how you feel about your actions and behaviors and how you see others.

7. Positive growth and resilience: The final stage is characterized by developing a more resilient ego. You are informed by lessons learned and have a

deeper understanding of your emotional needs and boundaries. You are learning to steer your ego, not the other way around, and you know what you need to recover from setbacks and new challenges.

Navigating through the stages of Masculine Betrayal Trauma is unique to each of us. It's important to explore each stage to process all your emotions and foster a greater sense of self. As you progress, you will start healing from the immediate pain caused by the betrayal and gain clarity about what direction you want to take in your life and who you want to become. The journey has its challenges, but you will be flexing your emotional resilience muscles during this time.

In the following chapters, we will explore each stage of the MBT Recovery™ model in depth, providing a breakdown and practical strategies to assist you throughout your healing journey. These chapters are intended to give you an understanding of the intricacies and subtleties associated with coping after betrayal. Ultimately, the purpose is to reduce the missteps and misunderstandings that limit you in your betrayal recovery process.

Chapter 6:

INITIAL SHOCK + EGO INJURY— STAGE I

The initial stage of MBT Recovery™ is shock and ego injury, which has a profound impact on both the psyche and the body. When you discover your partner's infidelity, you experience primarily the physiological reaction of shock. In scientific terms, the shock can be understood as the body's acute stress response—the "fight or flight" response. Your body releases stress hormones like adrenaline and cortisol, which prepare you to either confront or flee from a perceived threat.

Physiologically, shock can manifest in increased heart rate, rapid breathing, heightened alertness, or even a feeling of numbness or detachment from reality. These mechanisms help you cope with stress or trauma. Mentally, shock often results in difficulty processing thoughts coherently, a sense of disbelief, confusion, and overwhelming emotional turmoil.

Here's where the ego fits in. The injury that accompanies the shock is closely linked to your sense of self and identity. It challenges ingrained beliefs about your role in the relationship and your perception of self-worth. You may feel anxious or depressed or have fluctuating moods, which can lead to denying or repressing the betrayal as a way of protecting your self-esteem.

PROCESSING THE SHOCK

Dealing with the shock is a jolt to the system—but it's not permanent. The shock of being betrayed is only part one of the journey toward healing, and during this part you are simply processing many feelings and emotions, trying to make sense of what has happened. You are just beginning to recognize and accept the emotional effects of the trauma. Your responses are natural, normal, and crucial in starting the recovery process. It's also important to know that your reactions, though intense, are not a sign of weakness but a reflection of how deeply you have been affected by the betrayal.

The shock doesn't have to control you. You can regulate your body's stress responses quite a bit by taking up calming techniques like breathing exercises, practicing mindfulness (bringing awareness to what you are experiencing internally and being in the present moment), or other gentle physical activities. These practices will help you feel calmer and more relaxed, more stable, and lessen the symptoms of the shock.

Mentally processing the shock requires giving yourself time and space to come to terms with what happened.

You are learning to allow yourself to experience a range of emotions without judging or rushing through them.

CHALLENGING NEGATIVE THOUGHTS

During this stage, you may find yourself grappling with limiting belief stories. These are stories the ego conjures up, and they often revolve around self-blame, inadequacy, or a perceived failure in the relationship. Recognize these narratives as natural responses to your ego's injury but also challenge their validity. Understand that these beliefs are often rooted in cultural constructs of masculinity. Seeing them for what they are—empty narratives—is a perspective that helps you to disentangle yourself from spiraling negativity and not buy into thoughts that lower your sense of self-worth.

The initial shock and ego injury stage is about understanding and navigating the immediate impact of betrayal. You are coming to terms with the trauma's physical and mental impacts and beginning to challenge the limiting beliefs that arise from your injured ego. This stage sets the foundation for deeper emotional work in the later stages of MBT Recovery™.

PRACTICAL ADVICE

1. Acknowledge your Feelings: Give yourself permission to feel the shock and all the emotions that come with it. Acknowledging these feelings is the first step toward processing them.

2. Seek support: Talk to trusted friends, family, or a therapist/betrayal coach. A support system can provide a much-needed outlet for expressing your emotions safely and receiving nonjudgmental advice and support.

3. Reflect on past experiences: Reflect on situations in your life when you've felt similar emotions and how you pulled out of them. Understanding how you've navigated past traumas can offer insights into coping with your current situation.

4. Journaling: Writing down your thoughts and feelings can help process the shock. Journaling provides a private space to express and make sense of your emotions. Writing can give you additional mental clarity that going over feelings in your head might not produce.

5. Limit exposure to the betrayal story: Visualizing the details and feelings of your initial shock can be

as real in your mind as if it was just happening. Continuously revisiting the details of the betrayal can even intensify the shock. You don't have to repress your feelings and thoughts completely; you just need to give yourself breaks from the story and find diversions so you can refocus on your daily activities and interactions.

6. Self-care: Focus on activities that promote well-being, such as exercise, healthy eating, adequate sleep, hobbies, and activities that you enjoy like watching a sporting event, cardio work or lifting weights at a gym, reading, gardening, or fixing yourself a nourishing meal.

7. Challenge limiting beliefs: Begin recognizing and challenging the limiting beliefs that arise. "I'm not good enough." "I'm too old." "I don't have what it takes to get through this situation." Ask yourself if these beliefs are genuinely accurate or if they are a construct and simply a reaction to the trauma.

8. Stay grounded: Practice grounding techniques such as deep breathing, meditation, or mindfulness to stay present and reduce feeling overwhelmed by thoughts and distractions.

9. Take time off: If possible, take time away from work or other responsibilities to process your emotions and focus more on yourself.

10. Plan for public reactions: If the infidelity is known publicly, plan how you will handle reactions from others to protect your emotions. Work out plans and practice what you will say in different scenarios.

This initial phase sets the tone for your healing journey. Don't underestimate the initial shock and its impact on your ego. It can disrupt the core of a person's identity: how you see yourself, questioning long-held beliefs, who you are, and your connection with others.

It is important to grasp and navigate this stage effectively, to gradually come to terms with the reality of being betrayed while also starting the process of separating your self-worth from your partner's actions. This stage can often bring turmoil, but it also presents an opportunity for deep personal reflection and growth. Here, you will redefine your understanding of your strength, vulnerability, and resilience.

The journey through Initial Shock + Ego Injury is unique for every individual and varies in intensity and duration. Some may linger in this phase while others may move through it more quickly. Regardless of the pace, knowing this process is vital to acknowledging and addressing the emotional upheaval. Use the practical strategies outlined in this chapter as a guide.

As you pass from stage to stage, remember that each is necessary for healing, understanding, and eventually, transformation. The journey through betrayal trauma is challenging, but overcoming challenges brings personal discovery and growth. By understanding and working through each stage—not trying to take shortcuts—you can emerge from this experience wiser, more determined, and with an optimistic and clearer vision of your future.

MY EXPERIENCE

One of my biggest revelations was the sheer magnitude of the shock that enveloped me, a reality I was utterly blind to at the onset of learning of my then-wife's betrayal. This shock wasn't a feeling of disbelief; it was like a massive wave that washed away my sense of self, leaving me lost in a sea of confusion and sadness. Looking back, I now realize that seeking therapy early on could have helped avoid some of the turmoil. However, at that time I felt paralyzed—not physically but emotionally—and unable to reach out for the help I desperately needed.

Adding to this struggle was a story I told myself that some of the closest people in my life who knew about my situation would no longer want to deal with my constant struggles and neediness. I convinced myself that I would only be a bother to them, which at times led me away from the support I craved and needed. My navigation through the initial shock was a journey that took me down the wrong path at times. I was caught in a vicious cycle of negativity, where I loathed the thought of physical movement or social interaction and started to eat to numb the pain. My retreat into isolation dug a chasm so deep that I often questioned whether I'd find my way back to the surface because my sense of self and pride was gone.

Amid all that chaos, my men's group emerged as a ray of hope during my moments of despair. Despite my reluctance to their check-ins and simple suggestions like grabbing coffee with another group member, their consistent support and love became a lifeline for me, guiding me back toward a sense of normality and healing that I couldn't have achieved alone. This period of initial shock and the subsequent journey toward recovery taught me an invaluable lesson: I realized that, despite the depth of my despair, we are never truly alone, even when we think we are.

If you feel surrounded by the shadows of loneliness, I implore you to take a step—no matter how small—to reach out. The barriers you perceive, whether they stem from exhaustion, fear, or self-doubt, are surmountable. Connect with a friend or a family member or seek professional guidance. The healing journey should not be a solitary one, and the belief that you're unworthy of care or that no one is there to listen is a fallacy. Pick up the phone, make the call, send a text, and connect with someone who offers comfort and a listening ear. It's the first step on a path that reaffirms your worth and strength to overcome. Remember, you are not alone in fighting this fight. The capacity for resilience and renewal lies within you and in your acceptance of the lifelines that are offered to you.

Chapter 7:

QUESTIONING SELF-WORTH— STAGE II

UNDERSTANDING THE SHATTERED EGO IN MASCULINE BETRAYAL

After experiencing betrayal, your sense of self can be deeply shaken, causing you to question your value and worth. During this stage, you might struggle over concerns about your attractiveness, sexual ability, and desirability as a partner. Your uncertainties can intensify with expectations about your worth and ability to maintain a relationship, creating an internal narrative that can be self-deprecating.

THE INTERPLAY OF EGO, SELF-LOVE, AND SELF-WORTH

Following partner infidelity, there's a significant interplay between the ego, self-love, and feelings of worthiness that often challenge core beliefs. The ego is often influenced by validation, and these core beliefs suffer a blow that extends beyond the relationship. This initiates an inward storm where deeper aspects of self-love and self-worth are brought into focus and questioned.

UNDERSTANDING CORE BELIEFS

Core beliefs are the fundamental convictions you hold about yourself, others, and the world. They are deeply rooted in your psyche and ego and are self-perpetuating. Often formed in early childhood, they attract evidence that makes them stronger, continuing to influence your thoughts, feelings, and behaviors throughout life. With regard to partner betrayal, core beliefs related to self-worth come under intense scrutiny.

- Core beliefs and the ego: The ego (the part of the psyche that experiences and reacts to the outside world) is heavily influenced by your core beliefs. It tends to equate a man's value with external factors such as success in relationships, social status, and the fidelity of a partner. A crisis of self-worth can occur when your core beliefs are threatened or lost in the betrayal process.

- Betrayal and reassessment of core beliefs: Betrayal forces you to reexamine your core beliefs. It prompts you to ask questions like, "Am I truly lovable?" "What makes me worthy?" and "Do I define my value or is it defined by others?" Reassessing can be painful but necessary if you want to realign your ego with a more authentic sense of self.

- Self-love and self-worth beyond society's expectations: This stage is about moving beyond society's expectations and redefining your self-worth based on internal values and self-love. Here, you're realizing that worthiness doesn't depend on external validation or your partner's faithfulness but is built into you.

PRACTICAL ADVICE

1. Identify and challenge core beliefs: Reflect on the core beliefs that have shaped your sense of self-worth. Challenge any beliefs that tie your worth to external validation. For example, question the thought that not having a successful relationship means you're not good enough as a person.

2. Embrace self-compassion: Practice self-compassion, especially when dealing with feelings of inadequacy or failure. Remind yourself that your

worth is not defined by the betrayal. Deconstruct the thought, "They betrayed me, so, therefore, I must not be worthy."

3. Cultivate internal validation: Shift your focus from seeking external validation to nurturing internal validation. Recognize and celebrate your inherent qualities and achievements. Your worth as a person is defined by you and no one else. What might happen in the world around you and the people who have entered your world does not negate being proud of the things you do and what you have accomplished. Celebrate what you bring to the world by being you.

4. Engage in positive self-talk: Replace negative self-talk with affirmations that reinforce your value and worth. Some examples: "I deserve to be happy." "I am grateful for everything I have in my life." "I am open to change."

5. Seek therapeutic support: You might have trouble articulating your feelings or removing some of the negative self-talk. Consider therapy or a betrayal trauma coach to help unravel, define, and reconstruct healthier core beliefs about yourself.

6.   Explore personal interests and passions: Engage in activities that you love and that make you feel good about yourself independent of your relationship status. Even a few moments of taking part in something you love doing can break a cycle of pain at least temporarily and give you a glimmer of a positive feeling that there is life beyond betrayal.

The journey through the phase of a shattered ego is about rediscovering and reinforcing your self-worth and self-love. It's a process where the pain of betrayal becomes an opportunity for personal growth. By reevaluating and reconstructing convictions, you can emerge from this ordeal with a more resilient sense of self, grounded in an authentic understanding of your inherent value. This phase sets the stage for connections in the future both with yourself and with others. In these interactions, your self-worth is no longer dependent on validation; it's now deeply rooted in self-love and acceptance.

NAVIGATING THE STRUGGLE OF SELF-WORTH

After partner betrayal, men often find themselves questioning their self-worth, value, and identity. You'll need to dive deep into your psyche to reflect on and challenge the ingrained beliefs and patterns that have shaped your sense of self-worth. This requires honesty, vulnerability, and a willingness to confront uncomfortable truths.

1. Reassessing core beliefs: At this stage, you must examine the beliefs you hold about your worth—beliefs that are often shaped by past experiences, society's norms, and personal relationships. Ask yourself how these beliefs have influenced your perception of your worth and whether they truly reflect who you are or if they are just reflections of external expectations and judgments.

2. Shifting from external to internal validation: A key part of navigating this crisis is learning to shift your focus from seeking external validation to cultivating a strong sense of internal validation. Recognize and appreciate your intrinsic worth, independent of others' opinions or actions. Find validation from within, understanding that your worth is not contingent on external factors like relationship status, career success, or social approval.

3. Redefining goals and aspirations: Betrayal can act as a catalyst for redefining your goals and aspirations. It is an opportunity to align your ambitions with a healthier understanding of

yourself and move away from goals that are solely driven by your desire for external validation or social approval. Set goals that resonate with your true self and that reflect your true values and passions.

4.   Identifying and changing negative patterns: Identify the patterns and habits that undermine your sense of self-worth. These might include self-critical thoughts, feelings of helplessness, people-pleasing behaviors, or staying in situations that don't serve your well-being. Recognizing these patterns is the first step toward changing them, paving the way for behaviors and thoughts that reinforce a positive and healthy sense of self.

Experiencing a self-esteem crisis and a shattered sense of identity after being betrayed can bring life-changing revelations. You are liberating yourself from needing validation from others and rediscovering your worth. This process lays the groundwork for creating an existence where decisions and relationships are guided by a strong belief in your own values and self-respect.

PRACTICAL ADVICE

1.   Self-reflection: Engage in introspection to understand the core beliefs that limit your self-

worth. Reflect on their origins and how they have influenced your life.

2.   Set realistic goals: Redefine your aspirations based on a recognition of your inherent value, moving away from goals solely based on what you think is expected of you.

3.   Recognize and alter negative patterns: Identify habits or behaviors that undermine your self-worth and consciously work to change them. Examples of negative patterns are overeating, neglecting your health, and keeping to yourself.

4.   Affirm and uphold boundaries: Use your evolving sense of self-worth to establish and maintain healthy boundaries in all your relationships. For example, emotions are each person's responsibility. Someone else can't be solely responsible for your emotional support and vice versa.

5.   Face your fears: Confront your fears linked to feelings of unworthiness and work through them. This might involve revealing or admitting to yourself or others what you want, don't want, or are sorry you did—you are purging the darkness you've been keeping inside you and welcoming the light of the real you.

6. Implement self-care practices: Introduce daily routines that show yourself you are worthy of paying attention to yourself and your needs. Practice being "in the now," list on paper or in front of a mirror your qualities you are proud of, express on paper how your day went or an incident that brought up pain or joy, and work on your physical body—getting it in tune as you tune your mental state.

7. Visualize a confident self: Imagine a version of yourself that fully embraces worthiness. Identify the characteristics of this version and strive to embody them in your current life.

THE FUTURE ANCHORED IN SELF-WORTH

A foundation rooted in self-love and self-worth will open doors. Life will become more genuine and satisfying, and you will be empowered to make choices and engage with others from a place of integrity and respect for your needs and boundaries. You will be interacting with the world and others, confidently embracing wholeness.

Rebuilding a shattered ego and nurturing your self-worth are needed to heal from partner betrayal. It is a journey of self-discovery and transformation where you learn to value yourself independently of social standards or your relationship status. You are laying a foundation for a future where self-love and self-worth guide your decisions and interactions, leading to a more fulfilling and authentic life.

MY EXPERIENCE

In the aftermath of my betrayal experience, I felt like everything I knew about myself no longer seemed true, leaving me to question "Who the hell am I?" The discovery of the betrayal plunged me into an identity crisis where my reflection in the mirror became unrecognizable echoes of the person I once knew. Thoughts like "What's wrong with me?" and "Will I ever measure up?" haunted me constantly, eating away at my confidence and pushing me toward sacrificing my boundaries to avoid being abandoned by my then-partner.

The blow to my self-esteem was devastating, reaching a point where self-love and respect seemed like distant ideals. I found myself relentlessly pursuing validation despite the deep-seated belief that I was fundamentally flawed and unworthy of love. This internalized sense of inadequacy was a form of what I call "betrayal-induced body dysmorphia." In other words, I was absorbed with what I perceived as flaws in my appearance. My self-perception was so distorted that I was convinced I could never be desirable to my then-wife—or anyone else for that matter.

Looking back on this phase of my life, I find it tough to pinpoint the moment when I started to feel better about myself. Maybe it was a gradual process that unfolded through time, introspection, and a commitment to personal growth. What I do know is that my journey from self-doubt to self-discovery involved confronting the pain, acknowledging the lies I told myself, and recognizing how I minimized my own suffering.

If you're currently stuck in a cycle of self-doubt and blame, I offer you understanding and support. The feelings of unworthiness and inadequacy you're struggling with don't define who you truly are. The choices that led to this pain were not yours; they were your partner's. Your value as a person remains unaffected by your challenges or perceived imperfections. This journey through betrayal is an opportunity for profound personal transformation. Embrace the process because it will lead you out of darkness toward becoming a more complete and balanced individual who is capable of growth, learning, and resilience.

Chapter 8:

ANGER AND PROJECTION—STAGE III

The journey through Masculine Betrayal Trauma often begins with a surge of anger. This intense and sometimes overwhelming anger is a response to the sense of pain and violation that accompanies betrayal. The anger is not only toward your partner or a third party involved; it's a reaction to your crushed expectations and shattered trust.

ANGER AS A PROTECTIVE MECHANISM

For many men, anger serves as protection. It is a shield against emotions such as hurt, disappointment, and sadness that are exposed by betrayal. This anger can be expressed in one of two ways: silently holding on to resentment or loudly expressing rage. It's the ego's way of regaining control in situations where you feel powerless and exposed. By expressing anger, you are temporarily reclaiming some lost power and assertiveness.

THE COMPLEX NATURE OF ANGER IN MASCULINE PSYCHOLOGY

To grasp the complexity of anger within the framework of masculine psychology, you must understand how social norms and expectations influence how men express their emotions. Society often associates masculinity with stoicism and toughness, which can discourage men from showing vulnerability or sadness. Consequently, anger often becomes the go-to emotion, masking underlying feelings of pain, disloyalty, sadness, and disappointment.

Social conditioning frequently creates a misconception that anger is the core emotion, rather than viewing it as a surface reaction to deeper emotional turmoil. When it comes to betrayal, anger can act as a shield, concealing vulnerable emotions of heartache and disillusionment. Recognizing that your anger is superficial and that there is more to explore under the surface is a breakthrough on your healing journey. At this point, you are ready to inspect, explore, and express your full range of emotional experiences.

Once you understand the role of anger in masculine psychology, you can develop coping mechanisms for the pain you feel. By acknowledging and addressing your underlying emotions, you are on a more holistic healing track. With this awareness, you can also improve communication and emotional connections in relationships, leading to more balanced and satisfying encounters with significant others. Anger after betrayal then becomes an opportunity for growth and emotional enlightenment.

UNDERSTANDING ANGER IN MASCULINE BETRAYAL

Recognizing how anger expresses itself after experiencing betrayal is an important first step in managing it and transforming its impact. Although anger is a natural reaction, it reflects a surface-level emotion, concealing turmoil under the surface. For healing to take place, you must address these emotions.

- Anger as a mask for deeper emotions: Anger is frequently a secondary emotion, arising as a response to primary emotions like hurt, fear, or sadness. In the context of betrayal, anger can mask these deeper, more vulnerable feelings. Recognizing this can be the first step in addressing the root causes of your anger.

- Family influences and patterns: Your understanding and expression of anger are often shaped in childhood and influenced by family dynamics. Reflecting on these patterns can give you insight into your current responses and reveal opportunities for developing healthier ways of dealing with anger. ("They were never good for you." "You are better off without her." "How dare they treat you like that?")

- Healthy vs. unhealthy anger: While anger is a normal and sometimes a healthy emotion, it becomes problematic when you are no longer in control of it, resulting in hostility and aggressive outbursts. Understanding the difference between healthy expressions of anger and destructive ones is the difference between staying emotionally upset, lashing out, and giving others a dose of the angry feelings inside you, which perpetuates a cycle of anger, arguments, and possibly alienation.

NAVIGATING ANGER POST-BETRAYAL

In the wake of partner betrayal, effectively navigating through feelings of anger is a challenge and a necessity. Be aware of signs and discover outlets into which you can channel your anger. Use it as a catalyst for positive change and emotional strength.

- Recognize warning signs: Become aware when anger starts to build up. Identify early signs to prevent explosive outbursts and allow for more constructive ways to handle your emotions.

- Express anger in a healthy way: Find healthy outlets for anger, such as through physical activity, art, or conversation. These outlets let you release anger without causing harm to yourself or others.

- Reframe your thoughts: How you perceive a situation greatly affects your emotional response. Challenge negative thought patterns to help you manage anger more productively.

- Develop anger management skills: Consider what it means to manage anger in a healthier way. Identify role models who handle their anger well and learn from their approaches.

PRACTICAL ADVICE

1. Self-reflect on anger triggers: Reflect on past instances where anger caught you off guard. Understanding these triggers can help you anticipate and manage anger responses going forward.

2. Improve communication: Work on ways to express feelings of hurt or sadness that lie beneath the anger. What is it specifically that is upsetting you, and how can you communicate that openly to others? Can you express your anger without blaming or intimidating the other person? Is there a way to resolve the conflict mutually? Can you address subjects without insisting on being right? Open expressions of thoughts and ideas can prevent misunderstandings and control anger.

3. Seek professional help: If anger feels unmanageable, seek help from a therapist or betrayal trauma coach. They can provide tools and strategies for better management of anger. They can help you with self-reflection and uncovering the roots of your emotional distress.

4. Mindfulness and relaxation techniques: Practices like mindfulness, meditation, or deep breathing exercises can help calm your mind and reduce the intensity of your anger. Long-term anger has consequences, including physical effects like high blood pressure and increased risk of heart disease.

5. Journaling: Writing offers you inner access to your feelings. It's a safe space that reduces anxiety as you consolidate scattered thoughts and emotions

in a visible place where you can express and process anger in your own private way. It can also help you identify patterns and triggers more easily.

EMBRACING ANGER AS A STEP TOWARD HEALING

Understanding and navigating the emotions of anger following a betrayal is an integral part of the healing journey. This process involves exploring the origins of your anger, recognizing it not as something separate from you and uncontrollable, but as a natural response to pain and betrayal. You can acknowledge anger without allowing it to define or consume you.

When understood and directed appropriately, anger has enormous potential for growth and emotional resilience. It's a catalyst that drives you toward constructive changes, prompts you to establish boundaries and assert your needs, and advocates for you in ways you may not have previously explored. The remarkable genius of anger is its transformative power as a tool for personal growth and self-awareness.

When you learn to navigate and manage your anger, you are building a foundation for resiliency. This stage of the healing process involves acquiring the skills and understanding to confront challenges with confidence and assurance. It's a journey that ultimately leads to a deeper understanding of yourself and your emotional landscape, equipping you with the tools to handle difficult emotions more effectively going forward.

MY EXPERIENCE

Exploring the depths of my soul, I've always seen myself as someone who doesn't typically harbor anger. However, after experiencing the shock of betrayal from my then-partner, I found myself caught in a whirlwind of unexpected emotions where anger emerged as a prominent force alongside deep sorrow. This rollercoaster of feelings felt like a ride that alternated between rage and sadness—without warning.

At first, my anger was aimed squarely at my then-wife, the architect of my pain. However, as the fear of losing her consumed me, my resentment shifted toward the person she betrayed me with. My fixation on him grew so intense that I started wishing ill upon him and even entertained thoughts of seeking revenge by revealing his actions to his inner circle and professional contacts. These dark thoughts showcased the extent of my fury while also keeping me stuck in an unhealthy cycle.

As time passed, I came to realize that holding onto anger toward him was ultimately detrimental to my well-being and in some ways, I was giving my power away to this individual. It became clear to me that while he played a part in this ordeal, the root cause lay elsewhere. So, my emotions of anger shifted between my then-wife and myself, causing me even deeper pain. I found myself trapped in a cycle of self-criticism, blaming myself for not seeing the signs of her betrayal and falling victim to her manipulation, deception, and our lost trust.

This repetitive pattern of anger was draining. During this experience, I started to discover the lost pieces of my broken heart. Unknowingly, this marked the beginning of the healing phase of my journey. It was a time of introspection and the slow, meticulous work of piecing together my broken spirit.

As I navigated through the layers of anger and grief, I realized that these emotions—though intense and often overwhelming—were integral to the healing process. They were not obstacles to be circumvented but pathways to deeper understanding and eventual peace. Embracing this turbulent journey allowed me to confront and eventually transcend the anger, setting the stage for personal growth and the reclamation of my inner strength. Little did I know that the work of healing a broken heart was leading me to a resurgence of hope, resilience, and a newfound capacity for forgiveness and self-compassion.

Chapter 9:

COMPETITIVENESS AND JEALOUSY—STAGE IV

Betrayal often triggers a whirlwind of emotions, where competitiveness and jealousy take center stage. This chapter explores the aspects underlying these emotions, exploring how the male ego becomes competitive and jealous as a way of coping. These emotions are intricate and multifaceted going beyond reactions to infidelity; they represent an internal struggle within men grappling with challenges to their self-esteem, identity, and social status.

The desire to "win" or prove yourself superior to the person involved in your partner's unfaithfulness is a force that can dominate your mental landscape after partner betrayal. Your response can usually be traced to ingrained societal behaviors related to masculinity, and they can intensify as you attempt to regain control and restore your sense of damaged pride. You can be led down an unproductive path where true healing and personal growth are overshadowed by the need to dominate or reclaim your lost honor.

During this phase of the healing process, you must understand the dynamics of your emotions.

Introspection and acknowledgment of your feelings are essential in the transition from emotional turmoil to personal growth and emotional stability. The following sections discuss the complexities of these emotions you are experiencing and guide you through this phase of your healing journey.

THE COMPLEXITY OF COMPETITIVENESS AND JEALOUSY

- Understanding your emotional response: Feeling jealous and competitive comes from your sense of loss and damaged sense of self-esteem. These emotions are not simple responses to the actions of your partner—they are deeply connected to how you perceive yourself. Overturning those feelings happens when you reach a point where your desire to regain your lost sense of valuing yourself outweighs those initial feelings.

- Influence of social expectations: Society demonstrates in many ways how "normal" men are expected to react when faced with betrayal. Reacting to those norms can intensify your feelings of competitiveness and jealousy. They can push you in the direction where you respond in ways that reaffirm your masculinity and social male status.

PRACTICAL ADVICE

1. Reflect on emotion sources: Understand the deeper reasons behind feeling competitive and jealous. Recognize these emotions often stem from hurt and inadequacy rather than superficial rivalry.

2. Shift focus to personal growth: Instead of competing against a perceived rival, focus on self-improvement. Set personal goals and engage in activities that foster self-growth.

3. Develop emotional awareness: Cultivate awareness of how social norms influence your emotions, and challenge these expectations.

4. Seek constructive outlets: Engage in activities that positively channel your competitive energy. Sports, exercise, creative projects, and succeeding in specific goals and pursuits can be healthy outlets that boost competition and self-esteem.

5. Foster self-compassion: Be kind to yourself during this emotionally turbulent time. Practice

self-compassion and remind yourself of your inherent worth.

6. Get professional support: Consider therapy or support groups for strategies to manage these emotions effectively.

7. Rebuild independent confidence: Focus on rebuilding your confidence and self-worth independent of the relationship.

MANAGING JEALOUSY AND COMPETITIVENESS

When dealing with masculine betrayal trauma, you have to learn how to manage feelings of jealousy and competitiveness as part of the healing process. While these emotions are understandable, given the circumstances they can become overwhelming if not properly addressed. Recognizing and navigating through these feelings effectively is key to regaining balance and moving forward. This section provides strategies that can help you understand, acknowledge, and constructively manage jealousy and competitiveness, transforming them into opportunities for growth and emotional maturity.

- Acknowledge feelings: Recognize jealousy and competitiveness as natural responses, but don't let them dictate your actions or self-worth.

- Reframe the narrative: Redirect your energy toward personal growth and self-improvement, focusing on what you can control.

- Find healthy outlets: Engage in activities that boost self-esteem without involving comparisons with others.

- Practice self-compassion: Remind yourself of your value independent of the betrayal.

- Seek professional guidance: A therapist, betrayal trauma coach, or support group can provide valuable strategies for dealing with jealousy and competitiveness.

- Build emotional intelligence: Develop skills to understand and manage your emotions for more clarity in responses.

TRANSFORMING EMOTIONS INTO GROWTH

As you work through jealousy and competitiveness in the aftermath of betrayal, it becomes clear that the goal is not just managing challenging emotions but using them as catalysts for personal growth. Doing so requires a deep understanding of the roots of your emotions, a willingness to confront them honestly, and the courage to channel them into constructive paths.

The process of understanding your emotions is a deep dive into the self. You unravel layers of your ego and examine how social expectations and personal experiences have influenced your responses to betrayal. This self-examination is crucial, as it allows for a more nuanced understanding of your emotions, transforming them from overwhelming forces into understandable reactions to a deeply hurtful experience.

As you learn how to effectively handle your emotions, you embark on a journey that goes beyond recovery—you are on a path of self-discovery and emotional growth. By understanding how feelings of competitiveness and jealousy arise, you start to break free from the limitations imposed by these emotions, and you can find ways to assert your value and rebuild your confidence.

This stage of the healing process is about laying the foundation for emotional strength. It's an opportunity to develop coping strategies and emotional skills that will benefit you long after the current situation has passed. By transforming these emotions into catalysts for growth, you open possibilities for more balanced and rewarding relationships both with yourself and others. Understanding and managing these emotions in a healthy way allows you to regain your sense of self momentarily and move forward on that positive path marked by greater emotional balance, self-awareness, and resilience.

MY EXPERIENCE

Competitiveness has always been a defining trait of mine, yet during the initial shock of betrayal, its impact felt surprisingly muted. Initially, my competitive nature didn't manifest in a desire to outshine my then-wife or her affair partner; rather, it drove a relentless internal critique. I would at times compare myself to the affair partner, which created a cycle of self-doubt and diminished self-worth. This period was marked by a persistent "woulda-coulda" loop. I fixated on their actions and my missed opportunities to prove myself, which only served to erode my self-esteem further.

As time passed, this negative pattern started to change. Through introspection, I came to understand that my real battle wasn't with my then-wife or her affair partner but with my own inner demons and limiting beliefs. This realization marked a shift in how I viewed competitiveness and envy. Rather than allowing these feelings to control me, I redirected my focus toward personal growth and self-improvement.

This shift in perspective was transformative. A few years post-affair, I embarked on a journey of self-love that led me to get in the best physical shape of my life, and I decided to go to grad school. Beyond physical or academic improvement, this phase of my life was about redefining my self-identity and regaining my power. It underscored a vital lesson that my value and self-worth are not dictated by external validation but are shaped by my own actions and self-perception.

This journey showed me that jealousy and competitiveness, when channeled positively, can lead to personal growth. It wasn't about outdoing others but about surpassing my limits, breaking free from old habits, and reshaping the story of my life.

I realized that the true battle with partner betrayal is won by overcoming the barriers I placed on myself and that real triumph comes from conquering my fears and uncertainties. This insight helped me heal from betrayal and prepared me to tackle future obstacles with strength and certainty.

Chapter 10:

WITHDRAWAL AND ISOLATION— STAGE V

THE SOLITUDE OF BETRAYAL

After experiencing partner betrayal, you may find yourself struggling with a sense of solitude. It's a solitude not from being physically distant from others but an emotional void that widens following the infidelity of a partner. This chapter aims to help you understand this form of loneliness, which is often concealed behind bruised egos and social obligations. We will explore the reasons why you withdraw from circles, hesitate to share your pain, and encounter challenges in finding support.

The solitude experienced post-betrayal is marked by feelings of abandonment, inadequacy, and an intense sense of loss. Betrayal shatters trust and corrupts companionship, at its core prompting you to retreat. Men particularly struggle as they face the stigma of being betrayed in the face of society's idealized notions of masculinity. You might find yourself engaged in battles of your own design, fearing judgment and internalizing the need to maintain an appearance of strength and resilience despite your exposed vulnerabilities.

Social expectations for how you should cope with partner betrayal can further intensify your feelings of isolation. There is pressure to uphold a façade of stoicism to avoid appearing broken or defeated. The pressure you feel at times to conform can make it hard for you to ask for help or express your turmoil. So, solitude can act as both a refuge from judgment and a prison for your internal struggles.

Coming out of solitude after experiencing partner betrayal requires confronting yourself. You are putting back together the pieces of shattered trust, questioning your self-worth, and reevaluating your damaging judgments. Although this introspective process may be painful, it's a necessary step in the healing process. This is your time to self-reflect, understand your emotions, and recognize the importance of connection and support.

UNDERSTANDING WITHDRAWAL AND ISOLATION DYNAMICS

- Ego protection and isolation: After being betrayed, your bruised ego can lead to social withdrawal. Wanting to isolate yourself can stem from fear of judgment, embarrassment, or feeling like you have failed in a relationship. It's a way to shield yourself from perceived harm.

- Fear of inadequacy: The reluctance to discuss your situation often comes from fear that others will see you as inadequate. You are expected to behave in accepted forms of masculinity and strength and this can intensify your fears, making it difficult to seek support or share your feelings.

- Lack of support: Also contributing to feelings of isolation is the challenge men face when trying to find support. It's common for you to feel that your pain and experiences of partner betrayal are not truly understood or adequately addressed by your support systems.

PRACTICAL ADVICE:

1. Recognize the importance of connection: It's important to acknowledge that feeling isolated after experiencing betrayal is a normal response. However, you have to accept the significance of connection in the healing process. Allow yourself support and companionship.

2. Find suitable support: Look for support groups or communities specifically tailored to addressing masculine betrayal trauma. Being among others who have gone through similar experiences can provide a sense of comfort and understanding.

3. Consider therapeutic intervention: As mentioned throughout this book, therapy or properly trained wellness coaching can help you explore and understand your feelings of isolation. A therapist can offer strategies to help you cope with your emotions and guide you toward reconnecting with others.

4. Reestablish social connections: Begin by reaching out to close friends or trusted family members whom you feel comfortable confiding in. Gradually rebuild your connections, making sure you surround yourself with understanding individuals.

5. Engage in group activities: Participate in community activities aligned with your interests. It will help you meet people with whom you share common interests and foster a sense of belonging.

6. Journal and reflect: Use journaling as a tool to better understand and process your feelings of isolation. Take time to reflect on your emotions

and thoughts and consider how you can gradually reintroduce yourself to the outside world and move away from secluding yourself.

7. Practice mindfulness and meditation: Engage in mindfulness exercises and meditation techniques to help cope with the emotions associated with loneliness. These practices help you feel more grounded and keep you connected to the present moment.

RECONNECTING WITH THE WORLD AROUND YOU

Overcoming solitude after experiencing partner betrayal requires patience, understanding, and self-compassion. While seeking solace in solitude can be beneficial for healing, prolonged isolation may impede your progress and personal growth. This stage of healing is pivotal as it involves reestablishing connections with others, rebuilding trust, and rediscovering the value of relationships within a community.

One essential aspect of emerging from seclusion is realizing that strength lies in being vulnerable. Acknowledging your pain and sharing it is not an indication that you are weak—it shows courage that you've chosen the path toward healing. Where do you begin? Break down barriers you have constructed around yourself, allow others to see the real you, and offer support to them in return. This is the essence of vulnerability and is a catalyst for forming connections within yourself and with those around you.

Coming out of isolation also entails seeking and forging paths to connect with others. You might join support groups where you can find solace and empathy through shared experiences, or you could rekindle friendships with a new sense of openness. You are creating spaces in your life where you can genuinely express yourself and feel heard and understood.

Seeking support, such as therapy or counseling, can guide you during this phase. A therapist or betrayal trauma coach can offer insights and coping strategies, help dispel feelings of loneliness, and steer you through the complexities of rebuilding trust and relationships.

Ultimately, emerging from the solitude of partner betrayal marks the beginning of a new chapter in your life—one characterized by resilience, emotional maturity, and a deeper understanding of the importance of human connections. Remember, the experience of solitude in the wake of betrayal is part of the journey but not a permanent state. With the right support, self-reflection, and steps toward reconnection, you can transform this experience into an opportunity for significant personal growth and a richer, more connected life.

MY EXPERIENCE

Withdrawal and isolation became my unwelcomed companions during my journey through betrayal. I retreated into solitude—not necessarily to be alone, but because shame held me back. It felt like sharing my pain with others would make me feel even worse. As days, weeks, and months passed, I learned how to hide my emotions and pretend to be okay on the outside while on the inside I was unraveling.

In my self-imposed isolation, my self-esteem and self-love were overshadowed by beliefs that I was too damaged to find or have true love again and not good enough even as a partner. This distorted view of myself thrived in my solitude, creating a façade so convincing that I started numbing my emotions. I often wondered, how many tears can one person cry?

Yet, this dark period paradoxically brought some clarity. I began to see small glimmers of light only by confronting some of these deep shadows of my soul. Opening up to those closest to me about my being stuck in this darkness marked a new beginning in healing and change.

This short poem by Ben Lorry resonates deeply with me: "Once there was a man who was afraid of his shadow. Then he met it. Now he glows in the dark." Through my journey, I had to meet and embrace the darkest parts of myself to rediscover the light within.

This stage, full of challenges ultimately taught me that the path to self-discovery often lies in the darkest of spaces. By facing my fears and allowing myself to be vulnerable, I found a resilience and strength I never knew I had, which helped me uncover a new self that was always waiting to emerge.

Chapter 11:

REBUILDING AND TRANSFORMATION—STAGE VI

Transforming pain into strength after experiencing partner betrayal is like working on a complex emotional puzzle. It's not simply about getting over the immediate hurt but digging deep into one's mind and emerging with a renewed sense of purpose and self-awareness. The pain you feel becomes a catalyst for challenging long-held beliefs and values, prompting you to reevaluate what truly matters.

When you first experience betrayal, it brings intense, unspeakable pain and a feeling of loss that can be overwhelming. However, within this phase lies an opportunity for significant personal growth. Although uncomfortable and difficult to deal with, this pain forces you to confront parts of yourself that may have been neglected or ignored. It brings issues and insecurities to the surface so you can address them. This internal work forges personal development and emotional resilience.

Betrayal can often lead you to reassess your life, priorities, and relationships. It raises questions about who you are as an individual, your values, and the nature of your connections with others. This introspection can be a powerful tool for transformation as it guides you toward living in a genuine way that aligns with your true self. It promotes a change in perspective, where your focus shifts from seeking validation from others to finding fulfillment and accepting yourself.

Resilience also plays a role in this transformative process. Being resilient is the ability to endure challenges and emerge stronger. Building resilience includes acknowledging the pain caused by partner betrayal and learning to coexist with it rather than resisting or denying it. This acknowledgment does not mean condoning what happened but recognizing its impact and using it as a stepping stone toward growth.

As your journey continues, new insights and understandings will unfold. You will develop a sense of self accompanied by an understanding of your needs, boundaries, and aspirations. You will have more meaningful relationships, a clearer sense of purpose, and a stronger connection with your inner self. This is what transformation is all about.

The path from pain to empowerment is a testament to your resilience and capacity for growth, which is possible in every individual. The journey will take you through moments of despair and onward toward self-discovery, proving that even during your dark nights of the soul, there exists potential for significant transformation and personal empowerment.

THE ROLE OF EGO IN REBUILDING THE SELF

As you embark on the path of transforming pain into power, the role of the ego becomes pivotal in the process of self-reconstruction. This is how your ego—often seen as a source of defense or vulnerability—can be reshaped and used as a tool for positive change. In the wake of betrayal, as your ego recovers from its wounds, it will redirect from guarding against further hurt toward welcoming personal growth and self-discovery.

- Ego and self-reconstruction: The ego, once bruised and defensive, can become an important ally in the process of rebuilding yourself. You are harnessing your ego's energy, not for defense or retaliation, but for introspection and constructive change.

- Redefining values and beliefs: Experiencing partner betrayal can prompt you to question and redefine your core values and beliefs about relationships. This reevaluation is a step toward developing a genuine and satisfying approach to life and interpersonal connections.

- Understanding personal success: The conventional notions of success and fulfillment may undergo shifts following partner betrayal. You might find yourself redefining what success means to you by moving from validations to more meaningful measures of fulfillment.

PRACTICAL ADVICE

1. Reflect on personal values: Take some time to reflect on your values. Look at how they align with your actions and decisions. Understanding what truly matters to you is important, and you must be willing to hold those boundaries as they pertain to your values.

2. Embrace new beliefs about relationships: Consider embracing new perspectives when it comes to relationships. Reflect on any changes in your beliefs on what you want and need in a relationship and strive for more fulfilling connections.

3. Seek meaning beyond the pain: Look for lessons learned and insights gained from the betrayal, and try to find meaning in the experience. Use them as stepping stones for growth and emotional maturity.

4. Invest in personal development: Jump into activities that contribute to your development, such as reading, exploring hobbies, or pursuing educational opportunities.

5. Cultivate self-compassion: Practice self-compassion throughout this journey. Remember that growth takes time, so be kind to yourself along the way.

6. Rebuild confidence: Focus on your confidence by setting goals and celebrating even the smallest successes.

7. Expand your support network: Remember to expand your support network by connecting with others who can offer encouragement and understanding. Building a support system consisting of friends, family, or support groups is essential to fostering and encouraging growth during the journey of transformation.

REALIZING PERSONAL GROWTH FROM BETRAYAL

The path through betrayal and the accompanying pain naturally leads to a turning point: the emergence of a renewed self. This transformation represents a shift where past hurts and disillusionments give way to a deeper comprehension and appreciation of your own being.

During this phase, there is a transition from enduring pain to embracing growth. Men often find that their painful experiences have equipped them with a refreshed sense of self. This newfound identity is less influenced by expectations and more shaped by truths and values redefined through the lens of their own experiences.

The resilience cultivated throughout this process encompasses bouncing back from adversity, growing stronger, and becoming more self-aware. What you will experience during this period is an enhanced ability to navigate life with a balanced perspective valuing both your strengths and vulnerabilities.

AN ONGOING JOURNEY

Hopefully, you understand that this transformational journey is an ongoing process. Your new sense of self is not a final destination but a foundation for continuous growth and self-discovery. It's about moving forward with a renewed sense of purpose, armed with insights gained from your life's most challenging experiences.

The journey from pain to empowerment demonstrates the strength and adaptability that lies within every human. Discovering a sense of identity after being betrayed becomes an asset in navigating life's intricacies with confidence and genuineness. This transformation is about embracing a deeper and more fulfilling existence.

MY EXPERIENCE

Looking back on this chapter, I can't help but notice how my growth journey is still evolving even after all these years. The further I have moved away from the initial betrayal, the clearer and wiser my perspective has become. The anger I once felt toward my then-wife and her acting-out partner has slowly turned into gratitude for the lessons learned along the way. Ironic, isn't it? Despite being one of the toughest periods in my life, it had also been incredibly enlightening and healing.

This experience compelled me to reevaluate what was working and what wasn't in my life, leading me to break free from a relationship and marriage that was hindering my growth. Through this process, I discovered that I am worthy of receiving love—from others as well as from myself.

You may find yourself feeling stuck at some point in your life without realizing it or knowing how to escape. Let me assure you that breaking free is both possible and achievable. I often advise my therapy clients that "change is inevitable; growth is optional." So, ask yourself, "What direction am I heading in my life and relationships?" "How do I wish to present myself to the world?" "Where might I be holding back my potential?"

For a long time, I played small, especially when it came to matters of the heart and expressing my feelings and truth. I would often surrender my power within my relationship. However, I have realized that if my partner is unwilling to accept my honesty or fight for our relationship, then maybe that path is not meant for me. Prioritizing myself was a hard lesson to learn that has been integral to my well-being. I chose me, which took a long time to realize was okay.

Chapter 12:

POSITIVE GROWTH—STAGE VII

The journey through partner betrayal and the resulting trauma is undoubtedly difficult, and it has the potential to bring about intense personal growth. For you, this path leads to the emergence of a more resilient version of yourself as a man because it is the catalyst for introspection that reshapes your understanding of who you are and your role in the world. As you progress through the stages of partner betrayal trauma, a new sense of yourself begins to take shape—one that is shaped by your new experiences and insights.

This transformative journey is alchemy, where the pain and turmoil caused by betrayal gradually transmutes into sources of strength and wisdom. Men can often find that their challenging experiences become catalysts for growth and self-discovery. Amid this upheaval, old perspectives and beliefs melt away, making space for understanding and a renewed sense of purpose.

FROM VULNERABILITY TO RESILIENCE

As you journey through partner betrayal, a newfound vulnerability can often become the initial response.

However, as you experience this vulnerability, you begin to discover a resilience that may have gone unnoticed. This resilience isn't about toughening yourself against emotions but embracing them as aspects of the human experience. You are learning to balance vulnerability with strength, pain with wisdom, and loss with growth.

As you develop this new sense of self, you might see a shift in how you define success. You move away from seeking validation and instead focus on personal fulfillment and authenticity. While partner betrayal can be a force that challenges your narrative, it also opens the door to self-reinvention and empowerment.

The emergence of this stronger version of yourself is proof of your resilience and capacity for transformation. It is a journey that pushes your core but also presents an invaluable opportunity for personal growth and empowered existence.

NURTURING GROWTH FROM THE ASHES OF BETRAYAL

In the aftermath of betrayal, you may find yourself at a crossroads that has the potential to bring about growth and evolution. This phase is born out of pain and disappointment, which holds within it an opportunity for introspection and self-redefinition. Amidst this emotional upheaval, the possibility to transform and grow becomes theoretical and tangible. This transformation is about taking the lessons learned from the pain and using them as a foundation for a stronger, more resilient self.

- Positive ego development: Despite the devastation caused by betrayal, it can serve as an opportunity for transformation of your sense of self. This involves transitioning from a defensive mindset to an open and secure understanding of yourself.

- Learning from the experience: The experience of partner betrayal, with all its emotions, becomes the teacher. It provides insights into your needs, triggers, and areas for development.

- Deeper understanding of boundaries: Throughout the healing process, you develop a comprehension and appreciation for setting your personal boundaries. This newfound knowledge plays a role in relationships and self-care practices.

PRACTICAL ADVICE

1. Embrace the lessons learned: Take time to reflect on the lessons derived from experiencing partner betrayal. Recognize how these lessons have

contributed to your growth and understanding of yourself.

2.   Cultivate emotional intelligence: Foster emotional intelligence by understanding and managing your emotions. This involves identifying triggers and learning healthier ways of responding to them.

3.   Reevaluate and set boundaries: Use this experience as an opportunity to reassess and establish boundaries within your relationships. Recognize the importance of setting boundaries to foster respect and maintain your well-being.

4.   Invest in self-discovery: Engage in activities that encourage self-discovery, such as keeping a journal, practicing meditation, or seeking professional help. These practices can help you understand your core values and identify what truly brings you happiness.

5.   Build a supportive network: Surround yourself with individuals who support and comprehend your journey. This may include friends, family members, support groups, or a therapist.

6.   Practice self-care: Make self-care a priority in your growth journey. Take care of your health and

pursue hobbies that bring you joy and sustain your emotional well-being.

7.   Stay open to new experiences: Remain open to new experiences and perspectives. This openness can lead to new opportunities for growth and fulfillment.

EMBRACING TRANSFORMATION THROUGH THE STAGES

The final stage of MBT Recovery™ signifies a rebirth— a culmination of navigating through the seven transformative stages. Often referred to as "The Resilience of Rebirth," this stage is not about recovering from the past but embracing a future shaped by newfound strength and wisdom. It symbolizes the result of a journey that's both challenging and enlightening.

Reflecting on the Seven Stages of MBT Recovery™, you will see a journey that begins with the shock and denial of betrayal and moves through the turbulence of anger and jealousy, the solitude of withdrawal, and the deep introspection of rebuilding. Each stage plays a crucial role in your overall process of healing and growth. Understanding these stages is vital for anyone navigating through betrayal trauma, as it provides a roadmap for the emotional and psychological terrain they will encounter.

1. Initial shock and ego injury: Managing the shock and impact on your self-esteem.

2. Questioning self-worth: Addressing deep-seated beliefs about your personal values and relationships.

3. Anger and projection: Learning how to process anger while redirecting it in constructive ways.

4. Competitiveness and jealousy: Overcoming feelings of rivalry or inadequacy through self-reflection.

5. Withdrawal and isolation: Navigating through periods of solitude and rediscovering the importance of connection.

6. Rebuilding and transformation: Utilizing this experience as a catalyst for growth while reevaluating your life's priorities.

7. Positive growth and resilience: Embracing a version of yourself with a renewed sense of purpose and understanding.

Recognizing and acknowledging your current stage in MBT Recovery™ is crucial. It not only clarifies the emotions and challenges you're facing but also aids in devising effective healing strategies. Each stage requires a different approach and coping mechanisms. Be aware of where you stand in this process to ensure effective recovery and personal growth.

MOVING FORWARD WITH INSIGHT AND STRENGTH

As you progress through these stages, reaching the final phase of rebirth can bring about a transformation. This rebirth is characterized by a deeper understanding of yourself, a refined approach to relationships, and a clearer vision of what constitutes true fulfillment. The resilience you acquire during this journey equips you with the tools and insights you need to face future challenges with a stronger, more adaptive mindset.

The path through the seven stages of MBT Recovery™ is a process of metamorphosis. It takes you from the depths of pain and confusion to heights of self-awareness and empowerment. Understanding these stages is integral for healing from betrayal and also a framework for a more resilient and fulfilling life. It truly demonstrates the resilience and flexibility of the soul, proving that after enduring deep betrayal, you can emerge reborn, stronger, and more empowered than ever before.

MY EXPERIENCE

When I think about growth, I realize it can happen at any moment in my life, no matter the circumstances. Looking back on my journey through partner betrayal, it almost feels like I'm recounting someone else's story. The person I am today is so different from who I used to be during those dark days, months, and yes, years. While I certainly wouldn't have chosen the pain I endured, it definitely made me a better father, friend, therapist, husband (for a second time), and man.

Life is about choices. Some you make yourself, and some are thrust upon you. I believe what truly shows your character and integrity is how you handle these moments. It's about the lessons you learn from these challenges and how you use those lessons to improve your life and the lives of those you cherish.

The betrayal I faced set me on a path that took me by surprise, eventually leading me to become a therapist helping men deal with similar life struggles and to write this book. One of the things I've learned is the importance of being vulnerable and humble. These qualities have not just transformed how I view myself; they have enriched how I connect with the world around me and the people in it. The changes that have stemmed from my betrayal experience have been both a blessing and a gift, showing me a new way of being. For that, I am a lucky man.

Chapter 13:

THE PATH FORWARD

As you reach the culmination of your journey through the pain of partner betrayal, you are faced with a decision: what path to take in your relationship or marriage and your life as a whole. In this chapter, we will get into the process of making this choice, whether it means ending the relationship or committing to its healing and rebuilding. This decision is deeply personal, filled with complexities, and influenced by factors such as personal values, the nature of the betrayal, and the dynamics of the relationship.

LEAVING THE RELATIONSHIP: NAVIGATING A NEW BEGINNING

When betrayal shatters the foundation of a relationship, you may find that leaving is your only or best option. Although this decision is incredibly difficult, it can be a massive step in your healing process. It marks an intentional decision to start afresh. Here are some things to consider:

Emotional considerations: Leaving a relationship post-betrayal involves physical separation and emotional detachment. This process can be painful and may bring feelings of grief, loss, and even relief. Allow yourself to experience these emotions fully as part of the healing process.

Legal and financial implications: If married, the divorce process can be complex. Considerations include division of assets, alimony, and legal fees. It's crucial to seek legal counsel to navigate these waters effectively and to understand your rights and obligations.

Children's well-being: If children are involved, their well-being should be a top priority. Decisions on custody, co-parenting arrangements, and how to communicate the changes to them must be handled with care and sensitivity. I urge you to choose your children first and not use them against your partner.

Rebuilding life independently: Post-separation, there's a journey of rebuilding your life independently. This involves establishing a new routine, possibly relocating, and creating a support system that helps in this new phase.

Social and community aspects: Managing the social implications of leaving a relationship is also necessary. Deciding how and what to communicate to friends and extended family requires careful consideration to maintain privacy and dignity.

Personal development and growth: Post-separation is your time for personal growth. Engaging in activities that enhance your well-being, seeking personal development opportunities, and perhaps exploring new hobbies or interests is empowering.

CHOOSING RECONCILIATION: THE PATH TOWARD RELATIONAL HEALING

For some men, moving forward involves choosing to stay in the relationship and working toward reconciliation. This decision requires a commitment to healing and understanding and often involves redefining the dynamics of the relationship. Here are a few important points to consider when working toward rebuilding that trust:

Establish and maintain boundaries: As you rebuild trust, you must have boundaries in place. These can include transparent communication, access to devices such as computers or cell phones, or specific actions that the partner who caused the betrayal should take.

Seek couple's therapy: Professional counseling can play a role in repairing your relationship. It provides a space for both partners to address the issues that led to the betrayal and develop strategies for rebuilding trust and intimacy.

Gradually rebuild trust: Trust is the foundation of any relationship. After experiencing partner betrayal, rebuilding it takes time. Reconstructing trust requires effort, patience, forgiveness, and a genuine desire to rebuild what has been broken.

Manage emotional challenges: Understand and manage triggers that arise for both partners. Be aware of these triggers and support one another through the healing process.

Communication and emotional honesty: Openness and honest communication are elements in reconciling your relationship. Express your feelings, fears, and expectations constructively.

Evaluate the dynamics of your relationship: Staying together often means reevaluating how your relationship functions. This might involve addressing imbalances, unhealthy patterns, or neglected aspects that may have contributed to the betrayal. Take these into account and work on them together as partners with sincerity so you can begin healing and rebuilding trust.

Take care of yourself: Prioritize your healing alongside the healing of the relationship. Individual therapy or a betrayal trauma coach can offer a space for each of you to address issues and emotional needs.

DECIDING WHICH PATH TO TAKE

Deciding to stay or leave goes beyond responding to the immediate pain caused by betrayal. It's a choice, a crossroads that will shape your well-being and the direction of your life far into the future. Each option comes with its own set of challenges and opportunities for growth and healing.

Moving on from the relationship: Opting to leave usually signifies a desire for independence and a fresh start. You will be working through the process of separation, addressing financial considerations, prioritizing the well-being of any children involved, and building a new life with a focus on making independent moves. Sometimes a difficult choice is what's most beneficial for your well-being and growth. You will have to decide that.

Committing to the relationship: On the other hand, choosing to stay is a journey of healing together within the relationship. It requires establishing boundaries, participating in couples therapy, working to rebuild trust, and redefining the dynamics within the partnership with more transparency than you had before, for a healthier bond. The emphasis should be on forgiveness, growth, and renewed intimacy, for starters.

Each decision you make requires considering your values, the nature of the betrayal, and the dynamics of the relationship. Ultimately, this decision is deeply personal and should be aligned with your long-term emotional and psychological well-being.

PRACTICAL ADVICE

Whether you lean toward leaving or staying, consider these suggestions to help you through this critical time:

- Seek professional assistance: As previously mentioned, therapy or counseling can offer guidance and insights as you navigate through separation or work on rebuilding your relationship.

- Build a support network: Rely on friends, family, or support groups for support. They can provide perspectives, comfort, and practical advice during this phase.

- Take time for self-reflection: Reflect on what you desire and need for your future. Consider your feelings about the relationship. Envision what you believe is possible as you move forward in life.

- Prioritize self-care: Focus on your well-being by engaging in activities that promote emotional and physical health.

- Consider the impact on children: If children are involved, prioritize their needs and well-being during this period of change to ensure they have stability and support.

- Look ahead: Whether you decide to stay or go, consider your long-term goals and aspirations. Think about how your choice aligns with your vision for the future.

- Maintain open lines of communication: Whether it's with your partner during the reconciliation process or with your support network as you navigate a new beginning, keep communication flowing.

Taking these suggestions into account, you can make a decision that addresses your immediate emotional needs and lays the groundwork for a fulfilling and healthy future.

EMBRACING YOUR DECISION

Reaching the point where you have to decide whether to stay or leave is a pivotal moment. This decision, often clouded by a breach of trust, takes the relationship into uncharted territory. You may struggle with the complexities and ambiguities of repairing what's broken or deciding if embarking on an independent road to recovery is too daunting.

The aftermath of partner betrayal may have you feeling confused and uncertain. Pervasive questions about the ability to rebuild trust, the future of rebuilding the relationship, and the emotional feasibility of staying or leaving become central in your mind. Early on, these decisions may seem insurmountable, fueling anxiety and a sense of indecision that can be overwhelming. Know that through time and putting the work in, you will achieve more clarity.

The social stigma surrounding betrayal adds another layer of complexity. Cultural narratives often depict leaving a cheating partner as the only acceptable choice, equating staying with weakness. This is an oversimplified perspective that fails to acknowledge the intricacies and personal nature of each relationship. Decisions are frequently influenced by expectations, which can overshadow your circumstances and emotional landscape.

Contrary to media portrayals and prevailing opinions in society, many men lean toward repairing their relationships after experiencing betrayal. The decision to stay and confront challenges to become stronger and more connected is often surpassed by judgments and misconceptions. It's not about cutting ties—it's about considering the depth of the bond, shared responsibilities, your emotional investment, and an honest assessment of the potential for mutual growth and healing.

Your journey working through this decision is deeply personal and can be influenced by considerations beyond your immediate emotional response to the betrayal. The complexities of your and your partner's intersecting lives—children, financial ties, and the level of connection—all play a role. Longing for reconciliation and a stronger connection after being betrayed can be what motivates you to overcome or not be bothered by outside pressures and personal challenges.

No matter which path you choose, whether it's rebuilding or parting ways, both options require courage, insight, and a deep understanding of yourself. Choosing to stay and rebuild is an act of bravery, a commitment to growth and healing in the face of adversity. Opting to leave, in contrast, embodies the strength of recognizing when a relationship no longer serves your well-being and courageously stepping into a new chapter of your life.

If you find yourself grappling with doubts or feelings of shame about your decision, remember that your choice reflects the level of your strength and awareness of your needs. You should seek support from those who understand the complexities involved in both paths and acknowledge the courage it takes to make such a life-changing decision. Whether you decide to work on rebuilding the relationship or embark on a new journey, know that your decision is valid, worthy of respect, and deserving of support and empathy. Remember that there is no one-size-fits-all solution when it comes to healing from betrayal. Each path represents a voyage toward healing and self-discovery.

The questions below are designed to help you reflect on your emotions and thoughts regarding your relationship after experiencing partner betrayal. These questions aim to bring clarity and insight, assisting you in making a decision that aligns with yourself and your aspirations for the future. Contemplate these questions and answer them honestly to gain an understanding of whether reconciliation and healing within the relationship are possible or to pursue a new beginning on your terms.

1. What are my profound emotions regarding the betrayal? How do they influence my thoughts about whether to stay or leave?

2. How has this betrayal altered my perception of the relationship and my partner?

3. Which values and aspects of the relationship are most important for me at this moment?

4. Can I envision a future where trust can be rebuilt? If so, what would that future look like?

5. How does staying in or leaving the relationship align with my beliefs and values?

6. What fears do I have concerning both remaining in the relationship and ending it?

7. How does thinking about leaving the relationship make me feel about myself and my future?

8. What are the potential effects on my growth if I stay in the relationship?

9. How do I perceive my role in the dynamics of the relationship? What am I willing to change?

10. What does a successful reconciliation mean to me, and do I believe it's possible?

11. If I decide to end the relationship, what are my aspirations and plans for my future?

12. How do I think others will view my decision to stay or leave, and how much does their opinions matter to me?

13. Do I have a support system in place for either choice?

14. How does leaving the relationship impact my emotional well-being?

15. What concerns do I have regarding how this decision will affect my children?

16. If I choose to stay, what boundaries and conditions must I insist on for me to feel secure and respected?

17. Reflecting on the relationship overall, what patterns or issues may have contributed to the betrayal? How can they be addressed?

18. How does this betrayal reinforce my understanding of love and commitment?

19. What have I gleaned from this experience? How will it shape my choices?

20. When I reflect on the past, which decision will bring me the most tranquility in five or ten years?

MY EXPERIENCE

In this chapter, I've talked about how many men, including myself, tend to react to partner betrayal by wanting to fix things. It's an instinct. Men are often wired to be problem solvers. Looking back, I can now see how I felt stuck and didn't have the tools to make smart choices that would have benefited me and my marriage.

Surprisingly, everything fell into place perfectly in the end, although often during the journey, things were bumpy and dark.

My initial objective post-betrayal was to salvage my marriage and "win" my then-wife back. However, as I've shared, this goal led me to compromise on maintaining my boundaries and not staying true to myself. My circumstances were complicated by a significant move across the country shortly after the betrayal was uncovered, leaving my then-wife and me separated by vast distance and multiple time zones as she remained close to her affair partner. This physical distance rendered it difficult to effectively work on our marriage, quickly causing things to revert to our old roles and patterns. This dynamic eventually became our new norm, and the issue of her infidelity became the proverbial elephant in the room that we didn't really address again in detail.

We continued like this for many years, and deep inside I knew the marriage was over as my clarity of what was next grew and my impatience of being stuck in a loveless marriage became too much to bear. I also no longer was willing to be convenient and just a placeholder or a husband with an asterisk for my then-wife. I realized that while my then-wife carried on with her life, including being with her affair partner, I found myself feeling stagnant, lonely, and lacking in both physical and emotional affection. I pondered the questions above, and ultimately, the answers led me to the decision to end the marriage for my well-being and to create a fresh start.

I vividly recall my trip back to my hometown to have "the conversation" with her about my decision to end the marriage. It was evident that she had some inkling of what was coming, and oddly enough I believe there was a shared sense of relief when I expressed my intentions. Almost immediately after our conversation, she informed her affair partner of the news, confirming that neither of us had been living in our truth. This decision seemed to have liberated us both.

If there's a message or lesson from my experience, it's that there is no timeline or guidebook for navigating partner betrayal and its aftermath or for deciding whether to stay or go. The key is staying true to yourself by heeding both heart and intuition. Ignoring that moment of clarity in my past marriage would have only delayed the outcome, leading to more pain for both parties involved.

Ultimately, choosing to end the marriage was about honoring my truth and choosing myself, a decision that marked the beginning of genuine self-expression and personal liberation.

Chapter 14:

MISSED OPPORTUNITIES

When someone betrays you in a relationship, it can serve as a reflection of missed opportunities for growth and improvement. It's important to remember that your partner's infidelity is not your fault. It is, however, an opportunity to consider any role you may have played in the dynamics leading up to it. This chapter explores these missed chances and how they can be catalysts for development and building healthier relationships in the future.

YOUR PARTNER'S RELATIONAL BAGGAGE

When you enter a relationship, it's common to bring your own set of challenges with intimacy, past wounds, and ingrained behavioral patterns. These challenges can manifest as fear of love, avoidance of closeness, love or sex addiction, or other complex issues. These preexisting challenges often come from experiences rooted in psychological issues that significantly impact how a relationship unfolds.

To fully grasp the dynamics of infidelity, you must understand the intimacy issues that often underlie the actions of the betrayer. These challenges are deeply ingrained within an individual's psychological makeup. They are shaped by past experiences that significantly influence their behavior within a relationship.

- Fear of intimacy: This pattern involves a subconscious fear of forming connections. Love-avoidant individuals may often feel overwhelmed by the closeness in relationships and, as a result, create emotional or physical distance. They may sometimes turn to infidelity to escape the perceived threat of intimacy.

- Sex or love addiction: People struggling with sex or love addiction often find themselves compulsively seeking out romantic experiences. This behavior serves as a coping mechanism for underlying issues such as low self-esteem or past traumas.

- Childhood wounds and attachment issues: Frequently, patterns of infidelity can be traced back to childhood wounds or attachment issues. Individuals may unconsciously replicate the patterns they observed or experienced in their lives, which may lead to dysfunctional adult relationships.

- Communication breakdown: A person who betrays their partner might lack the communication skills to express dissatisfaction or unmet needs within the relationship. This deficiency can drive them toward seeking fulfillment outside of their partnership.

- Emotional disconnection: In some cases, the person who betrays their partner may feel emotionally disconnected from them. This disconnection can stem from relationship issues or even their emotional unavailability. It drives them toward pursuing intimacy or connection elsewhere.

UNDERSTANDING THE BETRAYER'S ROLE

Exploring a betrayer's role in a relationship requires a deep dive into their psychological and emotional landscape. It involves looking beyond the act of infidelity itself to understand the underlying motives and unaddressed issues that led to such a decision as just discussed.

To fully grasp your betrayer's role in the dynamics of infidelity, you must explore the complex interplay of their emotional and psychological states. This exploration goes beyond the surface-level actions of infidelity to unearth the deeper, often concealed motives and unresolved issues that precipitated their decision to betray.

- Recognize past traumas: Many individuals who betray their partners carry traumas from their past, which greatly impact their behavior in relationships. These traumas may stem from experiences during childhood, previous romantic involvements, or other significant life events. The influence of these issues often becomes evident through relationship patterns, including a tendency toward infidelity. Addressing these traumas is not solely about understanding their role in the betrayal but also about initiating a healing and transformation process for you, the person who was betrayed.

- Identify coping mechanisms: A vital aspect of understanding your betrayer's actions involves recognizing how they cope with challenges. Often engaging in behaviors like seeking validation outside the relationship, having affairs, or emotionally distancing themselves from you are ways they deal with rooted insecurities, unfulfilled emotional needs, or unresolved psychological issues. These are defense mechanisms that act as a barrier against vulnerability. They are often rooted in a fear of getting close to others or an underlying sense of not being good enough.

- Reflect on relationship dynamics: Your betrayer's actions inevitably affect the dynamics of the relationship. Their difficulties with intimacy— whether shown through unavailability, avoidance, or addiction—influence their emotional well-being and the overall health of the relationship. Your betrayer needs to take time to think about how their behavior has impacted your trust, communication, and emotional connection within the relationship.

- Take personal responsibility: Your betrayer needs to accept responsibility for their actions. Recognizing that they chose to be unfaithful, regardless of the underlying reasons, is essential. This acknowledgment marks a step in the journey toward healing and making amends with themselves and you.

- Impact on the betrayed partner: Betrayers need to acknowledge and understand the impact their actions have had on you. Your feelings of betrayal hurt, and shattered trust are the consequences of their actions. This realization can be painful but is necessary to fully grasp the extent of the damage caused by the infidelity.

FOR THE BETRAYAL PARTNER: UNDERSTANDING IT WASN'T YOUR FAULT

For the partner who has experienced betrayal, it's important to grasp the range of factors contributing to your partner's actions as part of the healing process. It's important to recognize that betrayal is an issue often stemming from their psychological struggles and unresolved personal challenges. This understanding is essential in realizing that infidelity doesn't reflect your shortcomings or failures. The betrayal originated from choices and behaviors made by your partner, which were beyond your control and responsibility.

RECOGNIZING YOUR ROLE IN RELATIONSHIP DYNAMICS

While it is important to acknowledge that you are not at fault for the betrayal, reflecting on the dynamics of your relationship can also be helpful. This isn't about blaming yourself but gaining an understanding of how certain patterns and behaviors may have contributed to an environment where issues remained unaddressed. Maybe there were signs of distance, breakdowns in communication, or unresolved conflicts that went unnoticed. Recognizing these aspects can provide insight into understanding your relationship as a whole.

You have to differentiate between recognizing these factors and feeling accountable for the betrayal. Your role in the relationship dynamics does not mean you are responsible for your partner's infidelity. Instead, your reflection should revolve around comprehending the interplay of interactions and behaviors between you and your partner and how these factors could have influenced the course of your relationship.

EMPOWERING YOURSELF THROUGH UNDERSTANDING AND REFLECTION

Engaging in this process of understanding and reflection empowers you as the betrayed partner. It enables you to gain an understanding of the relationship dynamics and your role within it, without shouldering the burden of guilt for your partner's actions. This clarity is key to your healing and for making well-thought-out decisions about your future, whether those entail rebuilding the relationship or moving forward independently.

By separating your self-worth from your partner's actions and acknowledging your part in shaping the dynamics of the relationship, you can start to heal from the betrayal and do so with a new perspective. Taking this approach means you are beginning to understand yourself and your own needs better, laying a foundation for relationships and personal growth in the times ahead.

LOOKING AT YOUR ROLE

As the partner who has been betrayed, it's essential to introspectively examine your role in the relationship dynamics. Often, signs of your partner's struggles with intimacy might have been overlooked, dismissed, or rationalized. This part of the journey involves understanding why you might have been drawn to a partner with these challenges and why you tolerated certain behaviors.

- Complacency in the relationship: One warning sign is complacency. Over time, you might have become comfortable with the status quo, even if it meant ignoring certain red flags or unmet needs. Complacency can stem from a fear of change, a desire for stability, or simply a lack of awareness about the severity of the issues at hand.

- Avoiding confrontation: Another aspect to consider is the avoidance of confrontation. Setting boundaries and addressing problematic behaviors require open communication and sometimes difficult conversations. You might have found it easier to avoid these confrontations, thereby allowing unhealthy patterns to continue.

- Attraction to familiar dynamics: There's also the possibility that these dynamics were familiar to you, perhaps mirroring relationship patterns witnessed in childhood or early life. This familiarity, even when dysfunctional, can sometimes feel safer than venturing into unknown territory.

- Understanding your wounds: Reflect on your wounds and insecurities. Were there aspects of your self-esteem or past traumas that made you more susceptible to staying in a relationship with someone who had intimacy issues?

- Fear of being alone: Sometimes, the fear of loneliness or the belief that a flawed relationship is better than none can lead you to tolerate behaviors that go against your better judgment.

- Unmet emotional needs: Consider whether emotional needs were not being met in the relationship, leading you to overlook your partner's problematic behaviors. Understanding these needs is important in identifying why you might have been drawn to and stayed with a partner who had pre-existing challenges.

PRACTICAL ADVICE

1. Self-reflection: Dedicate time to reflect on why you were attracted to and tolerated certain

behaviors in your partner. This might involve journaling or discussing your thoughts with a therapist.

2.   Seek therapy or coaching: Counseling can be invaluable in exploring your patterns, childhood experiences, and emotional needs that influenced your choice of a partner and response to their behavior.

3.   Learn about boundaries: Educate yourself about healthy boundaries in relationships. Understanding what healthy boundaries look like can help you identify where they may have been lacking in your past relationships.

4.   Explore your fears: Be honest with yourself about your fears—whether it's the fear of change, confrontation, or loneliness. Addressing these fears is key to not repeating the same patterns in future relationships.

5.   Develop self-compassion: Practice self-compassion as you navigate this introspective process. It's easy to fall into the trap of blaming yourself.

Remember that recognizing your role in a relationship dynamic is not about blaming yourself but rather gaining insights for growth.

- Embrace change: Stay open-minded and embrace the idea that change is part of personal growth and how we approach relationships. Recognizing this can empower you to make healthier choices moving forward.

- Prioritize your healing journey: Make your healing a top priority. This may involve addressing past traumas, building self-esteem, or simply learning to be more present and mindful in your relationships.

- Engage in positive activities: Engaging in activities that promote self-awareness and personal development can be incredibly beneficial. Consider practicing mindfulness techniques, pursuing hobbies you enjoy, or even taking courses focused on growth and building relationship skills.

- Cultivate a supportive network: Surround yourself with supportive friends, family members, or communities that encourage healthy relationships and personal development.

- Plan for future relationships: Take the insights gained from this process into consideration when approaching future relationships. By understanding your past experiences, you can shape more fulfilling connections in the future.

By diving into these practices, you can start unraveling the complex dynamics of relationships and your role within them. Your goal is to become more self-aware and emotionally intelligent because these qualities will better equip you for relationships going forward.

Understanding and addressing missed opportunities in a relationship post-betrayal can be challenging yet enlightening. It provides a chance to grow as an individual and learn valuable lessons for future relationships. By acknowledging and working through these areas, you can emerge stronger, more aware, and better equipped to be a healthier partner in your current or future relationship.

MY EXPERIENCE

Writing this chapter was quite a challenge for me. Coming to terms with my role in the breakdown of my past marriage meant confronting truths I had avoided and had not wanted to voice for many years. Depending on where you are in your healing process or journey toward forgiveness or end of the relationship, acknowledging and taking responsibility for your part in the relationship breakdown can be incredibly tough yet vitally important to your growth and healing.

For years, I held on to the belief that I was the victim, finding comfort in blaming my then-wife for the pain caused by her betrayal. It felt easier to stay in that place of hurt, sometimes pointing fingers at her to justify my emotions. However, the comfort provided by my victimhood was fleeting, and the pursuit of healing truly demands a more honest self-assessment.

I must admit, part of me sensed my then-wife pulling away from me, and yet, I chose not to act. My tendency to downplay my presence in our marriage, not expressing my feelings, and failing to set boundaries stemmed from a deep-seated fear of being abandoned. This fear had been present before her affair and was rooted in my own lack of self-acceptance and self-worth. Despite putting up a front of confidence, I often felt trapped by my insecurities.

Additionally, I prioritized other aspects of my life over my marriage, subtly showing my then-wife that I wasn't fully committed to our relationship. This lack of effort was not lost on her, and it mirrored what I judged to be her own reluctance to fight for our union.

My avoidance of my truth and real engagement in our marriage was partly due to fear of vulnerability. In my clinical practice, I often hear betrayers state that they need to have a backup plan because being fully committed is frightening (fear of vulnerability), and looking back, I would guess that my then-wife did the same thing as did I in many ways. I convinced myself that it was better to shield myself from this issue to avoid any potential pain, but this avoidance only deepened and made our disconnection worse.

Through this experience I've learned a vital truth: I deserve love, and my needs and boundaries matter. Now I recognize that I subconsciously chose a partner who was in some ways emotionally unavailable like me, reflecting my own reluctance to fully invest in the relationship. The journey to uncovering my truth and valuing myself was difficult, yet ultimately fulfilling.

Today, I am in a loving relationship where I feel secure, not only because of who my partner is but also as a result of the personal growth work I've done. I found a sense of security within myself that shows how much I've grown by confronting my past, accepting my vulnerabilities, and working on my own self-development.

Focusing on healing myself has allowed me to form relationships built on genuine connection and respect. This new phase of my life is characterized by openness and honesty that were lacking before. I've learned how to set boundaries that reflect my values and enable me to engage in supportive, fulfilling relationships. This journey wasn't about recovering from betrayal but embracing vulnerability as a strength rather than a weakness.

Chapter 15:

SUPPORT AND RESOURCES

EMBRACING A HOLISTIC APPROACH TO HEALING

It's essential to understand that the path to healing and recovery goes beyond what you'll find in these chapters. While this book aims to offer insights and guidance, true healing often requires a multifaceted approach—that is, taking care of yourself, seeking therapy or betrayal trauma coaching, engaging in healthy activities, and building a support system. This chapter serves as your guide, pointing you toward resources to assist you on your healing and personal growth journey.

THE POWER OF COMPREHENSIVE SELF-CARE

When dealing with the challenges of partner betrayal trauma, self-care becomes an integral part of the healing process. Beyond indulgence, it involves nurturing your physical, mental, and emotional well-being. Self-care can take many forms, from finding solace in a comforting book to participating in activities that rejuvenate both your body and mind. In this chapter, I present self-care tools and strategies carefully selected for their potential to support your development and emotional well-being.

THE ROLE OF PROFESSIONAL THERAPY AND COACHING

While the support of friends and loved ones is invaluable, there are occasions when seeking guidance becomes necessary. Engaging in therapy or betrayal coaching with a professional provides an environment to explore your emotions, confront the pain caused by betrayal, and develop effective coping strategies. These professionals offer insights and techniques that have been honed through years of research and experience tailored specifically to help you process the trauma and move forward. Within this chapter, you will find references to therapists and counseling services specializing in supporting individuals dealing with betrayal trauma.

CHOOSING HEALTHY ACTIVITIES

Incorporating activities into your healing journey is a vital aspect of your healing journey. Engaging in activities that promote well-being, clarity, and emotional release can be powerful tools for rebuilding your sense of self. Whether it's participating in a sport, pursuing creative outlets, or practicing mindfulness through meditation or yoga, find activities that serve as outlets for stress and pain while fostering resilience and inner strength.

BUILDING A SUPPORT NETWORK

We all need support in the aftermath of betrayal. Isolation is not conducive to healing, so building a support network is crucial during this time. This network may consist of friends and family members and can also extend to support groups or online platforms where you can connect with others who have experienced similar challenges. Communities like these can provide a sense of understanding, empathy, and shared experiences, reminding you that you're not alone on your journey.

12-STEP PROGRAMS AND GROUPS

- *12-step programs*: Many people find solace in structured 12-step programs that offer support and guidance in healing from betrayal trauma. These groups bring together individuals who understand the challenges you're facing and create a space for shared experiences and personal growth. I understand if your initial thought is why you should go to a 12-step meeting when your partner has the problem. Well, I can tell you that these meetings give you the chance to realize you are not alone, and they are a great way to guide you through the healing process while having a group on your side. There are a handful of different 12-step programs that might fit what you are going through: S-Anon (for those in a relationship with a sex addict), COSA (for those in a relationship with a sex addict to help look at any codependency or what could be called co-addiction), Al-Anon (for family and friends of alcoholics), Recovery Couples Anonymous (for couples dealing with various addictions), and Infidelity Survivors Anonymous (a support group for individuals who have experienced infidelity).

- *Men's groups (MKP—The Mankind Project)*: MKP is a nonprofit/charitable organization that offers men an opportunity to dive into deeper aspects of their lives. It fosters growth, emotional intelligence, and understanding within a community environment. [mankindproject.org]

THERAPISTS AND BETRAYAL TRAUMA COACHES

Seeking support from therapists or betrayal trauma coaches can play a critical role in navigating the complexities of betrayal. Here are good places to start your search.

THE BETRAYAL SHRINK:

My website is full of information for men navigating betrayal. I have blogs on current topics, different ways for you to connect with me, and, if needed, information on how to work with me as you navigate these trying times: [BetrayalShrink.com] or feel free to email me at Adam@BetrayalShrink.com

ASSOCIATION OF PARTNERS OF SEX ADDICTS TRAUMA SPECIALISTS (APSATS):

APSATS provides specialized training to professionals for working with partners of sex addicts, ensuring empathetic, informed support with a focus on working with individuals navigating betrayal trauma. [apsats.org]

PSYCHOLOGY TODAY DIRECTORY:

An extensive directory of therapists allows you to find a professional specializing in betrayal trauma and related issues in your area. [psychologytoday.com/us/therapists]

INTERNATIONAL INSTITUTE FOR TRAUMA AND ADDICTION SPECIALIST:

IITAP is a renowned, for-profit organization offering training and certification for mental health professionals in treating sexual addiction, partner trauma, and compulsive behaviors. It's grounded in Dr. Patrick Carnes' pioneering work and his 30 Task Model. [iitap.com]

BOOKS AND WORKBOOKS

Below is a list of books and workbooks offering insights and guidance on dealing with relationship betrayal. It includes a range of perspectives to support and guide you. The books are listed in no particular order, and this compilation is not exhaustive. There are many other valuable reading options available that offer support and information on this topic. This list is a general guide and should be used as a starting point for exploring the wealth of resources available for those seeking help and understanding in navigating relationship betrayals.

- *The Intimacy Factor* by Pia Mellody—Mellody shares her insights from over 20 years as a counselor, focusing on achieving and maintaining true intimacy and trust in vital relationships.

- *The State of Affairs* by Esther Perel—Perel provides a comprehensive look into the complexities of love and desire and the impact of infidelity on relationships.

- *Mending a Shattered Heart* by Stefanie Carnes, Ph.D.—Carnes offers guidance for those grappling with a partner's infidelity, helping readers discern between bad behavior and sex addiction.

- *For Love and Money* by Debra Kaplan—Kaplan explores sexual and financial betrayal in relationships, combining her Wall Street experience with her work as a licensed psychotherapist.

- *Your Sexually Addicted Spouse* by Barbara Steffens and Marsha Means—This book offers a new perspective on the partners of sexually addicted individuals, framing them as victims of post-traumatic stress rather than codependents.

- *Ambushed by Betrayal* by Allan J. Katz and Michele Saffier—Katz and Saffier present a self-guided healing process for those experiencing betrayal trauma in relationships.

- *Leave a Cheater, Gain a Life* by Tracy Schorn—Schorn's guide focuses on the needs of individuals who have been cheated on, offering advice and satirical cartoons for those looking to rebuild their lives after infidelity.

- *Facing Codependence* by Pia Mellody—This book outlines Mellody's approach to identifying and recovering from codependent behaviors stemming from childhood abuse.

- *Unleashing Your Power* by Carol Juergensen Sheets and Christine Turo-Shields—A workbook aimed at helping those betrayed in relationships navigate through their trauma and regain a sense of self.

- *Prodependence* by Robert Weiss—Weiss introduces a new model for helping those caring for addicts, focusing on attachment and the concept that one can never love too much.

- *Intimate Treason* by Claudia Black—Black provides a guidebook for partners affected by sex addiction, focusing on developing healthy boundaries and making positive changes.

- *A Partner's Guide to Truth and Healing* by John Sternfels, LPC—Sternfels offers a pathway to understanding and healing for partners who have experienced infidelity.

- *Should I Stay or Should I Go?* by Lundy Bancroft and Jac Patrissi—This guide helps individuals in challenging relationships distinguish between healthy difficulties and truly problematic dynamics.

- *Facing Heartbreak* by Stefanie Carnes, PhD, Mari A. Lee, LMFT, and Anthony D. Rodriguez, LCSW—The authors use real-life stories and practical advice to guide partners of sex addicts through a process of recovery based on Dr. Patrick Carnes' model.

- *Moving Beyond Betrayal* by Vicki Tidwell—Tidwell provides a detailed guide on creating and maintaining boundaries for people affected by their partner's addictive behavior.

- *The Betrayal Bond* by Patrick Carnes, Ph.D.— Carnes explores the formation and impact of trauma bonds in exploitative relationships and offers steps for extricating from them.

- *I Love You But I Don't Trust You* by Mira Kirshenbaum—Kirshenbaum's book is a guide for rebuilding trust in relationships, regardless of the nature of the betrayal.

- *An Affair of the Mind* by Laurie Hall—Hall's book reveals the subversive side of pornography addiction and offers comfort and action plans for women in such situations.

- *The Betrayal Bind* by Michelle Mays, LPC, CSAT-S—Mays' book focuses on how a partner's attachment system functions in the wake of sexual betrayal and connects the dots from research to the lived experience of betrayed partners.

- *Help.Them.Heal.* by Carol Juergensen Sheets, LCSW, CSAT, CCPS-S, CPC-S, PCC—Sheets explores and shares a roadmap for couples to find their way back to each other after partner betrayal.

Chapter 16:

A SUMMARY THROUGH MASCULINE BETRAYAL TRAUMA

As we conclude our exploration into the depths of Masculine Betrayal Trauma, it's imperative to reflect on the journey from the initial shock of betrayal to the eventual renewal of self and spirit. This summary chapter aims to extract the essence of each section of our discussion, emphasizing the pivotal lessons and strategies that will aid your recovery and growth.

THE ONSET OF TRAUMA

The impact of betrayal is jarring, striking like a sudden blow that shatters trust and undermines your sense of reality. The initial response is often one of shock, a psychological paralysis that leaves you reeling from the unexpected revelation. This stage is fraught with confusion, pain, and disbelief, making it difficult to process emotions or think clearly. Recognizing and acknowledging these feelings as normal reactions to an abnormal event are necessary for setting the groundwork for healing. This period requires a gentle approach to your self-care, and physical and emotional rest are particularly important.

NAVIGATING EMOTIONAL TURMOIL

Following the shock, a storm of emotions typically ensues—with anger, sadness, and confusion swirling together. This phase requires cultivating emotional intelligence, a critical skill that involves recognizing and naming each emotion, understanding its origin, and learning how to express it constructively. Techniques such as journaling, therapy, and mindfulness are invaluable here in helping you channel your emotions into pathways that foster healing rather than destruction. As you navigate your emotions, try not to suppress your feelings but rather understand and manage them to rebuild inner peace.

RECONSTRUCTING SELF-WORTH

Betrayal cuts deep into the fabric of your self-esteem, prompting a painful introspection that might reveal long-buried insecurities and doubts. This reassessment is not a critique of yourself but about rediscovering your value and worth independent of getting validation externally. Practice exercises designed to redefine your self-worth, such as the Emotional Inventory, which can encourage a thorough examination of your strengths and vulnerabilities. Ask yourself questions that probe the depths of self-valuation to help you clarify how much of your self-image has been influenced by the relationship and how much truly reflects your individual essence.

OVERCOMING JEALOUSY AND RESENTMENT

Jealousy and resentment are common byproducts of betrayal, each stemming from a sense of loss and injustice. Overcoming these feelings is pivotal, as they can tether you to the past and hinder your progression toward healing. Understanding the roots of these emotions involves deep introspection and acknowledgment of personal pain points. Using strategies can transform jealousy into a drive for personal growth rather than focusing on others. This part of the journey challenges you to redirect energy from resentment to self-improvement and empowerment.

THE ROLE OF SUPPORT SYSTEMS

The path of recovery is seldom walked alone. The role of support systems—therapists, betrayal trauma coaches, support groups, and understanding peers—is indispensable. These networks provide emotional solace and practical advice and perspectives that may be obscured by personal turmoil. Selecting the right support system is essential, so surround yourself with people who provide positive influences and constructive feedback.

EMBRACING THE LESSONS LEARNED

Every experience of this journey, marked by its trials and revelations, holds important lessons about personal resilience and the human capacity for renewal. Reflecting on these lessons turns experiences into wisdom. This stage invites you to see beyond the immediate pain of betrayal to recognize the growth and strength that often follow deep emotional challenges. Here, you will find a renewed sense of purpose and a clearer understanding of what you truly value in relationships and life.

LOOKING AHEAD: REBUILDING AND MOVING FORWARD

The future after betrayal can be daunting yet hopeful. Setting new goals and establishing healthier relationships are necessary steps toward a fulfilled life. This future-focused outlook emphasizes redefining your successes and fulfillment beyond the shadow of your past experiences. It encourages proactive behaviors in crafting a life that reflects your true self, free from the constraints of past hurts.

CONSOLIDATING OUR JOURNEY

Your journey through the landscape of Masculine Betrayal Trauma underscores the resilience and potential for growth inherent in every man. This final reflection is a celebration of the steps you took toward healing and your affirmation of the continued journey ahead. The lessons imparted throughout the book aim mend and transform, offering a roadmap for you and others who find themselves on similar paths.

In this book, we have traversed from the dark initial moments of shock to the empowering stages of acceptance and growth. Each new chapter builds upon the previous chapter, crafting a roadmap for resilience that acknowledges the unique challenges you face in the aftermath of betrayal. As we conclude, I hope you can reflect on how far you've come and how the principles discussed here can continue to guide you. Your journey of healing and growth is evidence of your strength and resilience and shines a light on the path ahead for others navigating their way through the shadows of betrayal.

SUMMARY QUESTIONS

1. Reflect on discovery: How did you initially react to the discovery of betrayal, and what does that reveal about your emotional priorities at the time?

2. Understand emotional impact: Which emotion was most difficult for you to manage following the betrayal and why?

3. Grow from grief: In what ways has the experience of betrayal served as a catalyst for personal growth or change in your life?

4. Reassess self-identity: How has your self-identity shifted since the betrayal? Are there aspects of your identity that you now see differently?

5. Look at values and beliefs: What core values and beliefs have you reevaluated or reinforced in response to overcoming betrayal?

6. Use coping strategies: What coping strategies have been most effective for you in dealing with the pain of betrayal?

7. Seek support: How comfortable are you with seeking help, and what barriers, if any, have you encountered in doing so?

8. Forgive and reconcile: What are your views on forgiveness and reconciliation in the context of betrayal and how have they evolved?

9. Rebuild trust: What steps have you taken or do you plan to take to rebuild trust in your relationships?

10. Vulnerability lessons: How has vulnerability played a role in your healing process?

11. Communication changes: How has your communication in relationships changed since experiencing betrayal?

12. New boundaries: What new boundaries have you established since the betrayal, and how do you enforce them?

13. Insight into triggers: What triggers related to the betrayal have you identified, and how do you manage them?

14. Future relationship expectations: How have your expectations of relationships and partners changed?

15. Role of masculinity: How has your understanding of masculinity and its societal expectations affected your healing journey?

16. Manage mental health: What steps have you taken to manage your mental health in the aftermath of betrayal?

17. Reflect on anger and resentment: How do you handle feelings of anger and resentment that arise from the betrayal?

18. Impact on family and friends: How has the betrayal affected your relationships with family and friends?

19. Personal transformation: What is the most significant personal transformation you've experienced during your healing journey?

20. Vision for the future: Looking forward, what is one goal you have set that was inspired by overcoming betrayal?

About **ADAM B. NISENSON:**
THE BETRAYAL SHRINK

K̲nown as "The Betrayal Shrink," Adam is a Licensed Marriage and Family Therapist and Certified Sex Addiction Therapist. He specializes in guiding men through the complex journey of partner betrayal trauma, drawing from both his personal experience with partner betrayal and extensive clinical expertise.

Graduating from Pacifica Graduate Institute with a focus on Marriage and Family Therapy, Professional Clinical Counseling, and Depth Psychology, Adam is dedicated to addressing issues such as partner betrayal, infidelity, and sex addiction. His approach is compassionate and honest, helping men rediscover their identities and reconstruct their lives with purpose. Adam's mission is to empower men to emerge more resilient and self-aware from these experiences.

Adam truly understands the deep impact of partner betrayal because he was there over thirteen years ago, when his world was shattered after his then-wife confessed to an affair. The ensuing grief, confusion, and overwhelming anger felt like mourning for a lost identity. This intense loneliness and sense of failure led Adam to realize the scarcity of resources for men in similar situations.

His salvation came from his men's group, which provided a supportive brotherhood and his own personal growth and therapy. This experience inspired Adam to become The Betrayal Shrink, focusing on helping men navigate the darkness of partner betrayal. His mission is to offer a guiding light to ensure no man must face this journey alone.

Rising from Betrayal: Empowerment and Healing for Men